WISDOM OF THE IDIOTS

**For further information on
Sufi Studies please write to:
The Society for Sufi Studies
P.O. Box 43
Los Altos, CA 94022**

Also by Idries Shah

Oriental Magic
Destination Mecca
Caravan of Dreams
The Sufis
Special Problems in the Study of Sufi Ideas
The Exploits of the Incomparable Mulla Nasrudin
Tales of the Dervishes
The Pleasantries of the Incredible Mulla Nasrudin
The Way of the Sufi
Reflections
The Book of the Book
The Dermis Probe
Thinkers of the East
The Subtleties of the Inimitable Mulla Nasrudin
The Elephant in the Dark
The Magic Monastery
Learning How to Learn
Neglected Aspects of Sufi Study
The Hundred Tales of Wisdom
Special Illumination: The Sufi Use of Humour
A Veiled Gazelle: Seeing How to See
A Perfumed Scorpion
Seeker After Truth
World Tales
Kara Kush
Darkest England
The Natives are Restless

IDRIES SHAH

WISDOM
OF THE
IDIOTS

THE OCTAGON PRESS
LONDON

Copyright © 1969, 1970 by Idries Shah

Requests for permission to reprint, reproduce, etc., to:
Permissions Department, The Octagon Press Ltd.,
P.O. Box 227, London N6 4EW, England

ISBN 0 863040 46 2

First Published in this Edition 1989

Printed and bound in Great Britain by
The Camelot Press Ltd., Southampton

Note:

Because what narrow thinkers imagine to be wisdom is often seen by the Sufis to be folly, the Sufis in contrast sometimes call themselves 'The Idiots'.

By a happy chance, too, the Arabic word for 'Saint' (*wali*) has the same numerical equivalent as the word for 'Idiot' (*balid*).

So we have a double motive for regarding the Sufi great ones as our own Idiots.

This book contains some of their knowledge.

CONTENTS

THE FRUIT OF HEAVEN

There was once a woman who had heard of the Fruit of Heaven. She coveted it.

She asked a certain dervish, whom we shall call Sabar:

'How can I find this fruit, so that I may attain to immediate knowledge?'

'You would be best advised to study with me,' said the dervish. 'But if you will not do so, you will have to travel resolutely and at times restlessly throughout the world.'

She left him and sought another, Arif the Wise One, and then found Hakim, the Sage, then Majzub the Mad, then Alim the Scientist, and many more...

She passed thirty years in her search. Finally she came to a garden. There stood the Tree of Heaven, and from its branches hung the bright Fruit of Heaven.

Standing beside the Tree was Sabar, the First Dervish.

'Why did you not tell me when we first met that *you* were the Custodian of the Fruit of Heaven?' she asked him.

'Because you would not then have believed me. Besides, the Tree produces fruit only once in thirty years and thirty days.'

HAUGHTY AND GENEROUS

The Sufis, unlike other mystics or supposed possessors of special knowledge, are reputed to be haughty. This hauteur, they themselves say, is only due to other people's misunderstanding of their behaviour. 'A person,' they say, 'who could make fire without rubbing sticks together and said so would appear haughty to someone who could not.'

They are also reputed to be generous in the extreme. Their generosity, they say, is in things which really matter. Their open-handedness in material things is only a reflection of their generosity with wisdom.

People who want to study the Sufi way often practise generosity with goods, in an attempt to reach a greater form of generosity.

However that may be, there is an entertaining story told of three generous men of Arabia.

One day there was a dispute among the Arabs as to who was the most generous man alive. The arguments went on for days, and finally the candidates were by general agreement narrowed down to three.

Since the supporters of the three were on the point of coming to blows on the question, a committee was appointed to make the final decision. They decided that, as an eliminating test, a message should be sent to each of the three men, in the following terms:

'Your friend Wais is in great need. He begs you to help him in a material manner.'

Three representatives were dispatched, to seek out these men, to deliver the message, and to report the result.

The first messenger arrived at the house of the First Generous Man, and told him what the committee had commissioned him to say.

The First Generous Man said:

'Don't bother me with such trifles – just take anything that you want from what is mine, and give it to my friend Wais.'

When this emissary returned, the assembled people thought that surely there could be no greater generosity than this – and hauteur, too.

But the second messenger, when he had given his message, received this reply from the Second Generous Man's servant:

'Since my master is very haughty indeed, I cannot disturb him with a message of any kind. But I will give you all that he has, and also a mortgage upon his immovable property.'

The committee, when they received this message, imagined that surely this must be the most generous man in Arabia.

But they had not yet considered the result of the mission of the third messenger.

He arrived at the home of the Third Generous Man, who told him:

'Just pack up all my belongings and take this note to the money-lender to liquidate all my property, and wait here a little, until someone should come to you from me.'

Whereupon the Third Generous Man walked away.

When the messenger had finished the task, he found that an agent from the market was already at the door. The agent said:

'If you are the messenger from Wais to his friend, I have to deliver to you the price of one slave, just sold in the slave-market.'

The slave had been the Third Generous Man.

It is further related that, some months later, Wais himself, who had been a member of the committee of judges, visited a house where a slave waiting upon him turned out to be his friend the Third Generous Man.

Wais said: 'A joke can go too far! Is it not about time that you were released from captivity?'

The Third Generous Man, who was a Sufi, said:

'A joke to some may not be so to others. Besides, I am – in conformity with law – working out my release by arrangement with my Master. It will only be a matter of two or three years before I am again free.'

THE CASKET OF JEWELS

The tale is told of a woman who was carrying a casket of jewels of various sizes to a jeweller's shop. Just outside the shop she tripped, and the box fell to the ground.

The top came off the casket, and the jewels were scattered everywhere.

The jeweller's assistants ran from the shop, to prevent passers-by from taking any of the gems, and they helped to collect them.

An ostrich, which was wandering about, ran past, and, unnoticed in the excitement, swallowed the largest and best stone.

When the woman missed this jewel, she started to lament, and in spite of looking everywhere, it could not be found.

Someone said: 'The only person who could have taken that stone was yonder dervish, sitting quietly beside the shop.'

The dervish had seen the ostrich swallow the stone, but he did not want blood to be spilt. Therefore, when he was searched, and seized and even beaten, he said no more than:

'I have not taken anything at all.'

While he was being beaten one of his companions came up and reminded the mob to be careful of what they were doing. They seized him, too, and accused him of having probably taken the stone from the first dervish, in spite of his denials.

This scene was proceeding thus when there appeared a man endowed with knowledge. Noticing the ostrich, he asked:

'Was that bird here at the time when the casket was dropped?'

'Yes,' said the people.

'In that case,' he answered, 'address your attentions to the ostrich.'

The owner of the ostrich was paid the value of the bird, which was then killed. In its stomach was found the missing jewel.

AHRAR AND THE WEALTHY COUPLE

Emirudin Arosi, who came from a family well known for its adherence to the beliefs of a sect of enthusiasts, met a sage and said to him:

'My wife and I have for many years tried resolutely to follow the dervish path. Aware that we knew less than many others, we have for long contented ourselves with spending our wealth in the cause of truth. We have followed people who have taken on themselves the responsibility of teaching, and whom we now doubt. We grieve, not for what we have lost in material donations squandered in ineffectual commercial enterprises by our late mentors in the name of the Task, but rather for the waste of time and effort, and for the people still in a state of subjection to deluded and self-appointed teachers, people mindlessly occupying a house run by two false Sufis, in an atmosphere of abnormality.'

The sage, whom tradition names as Khwaja Ahrar, the Lord of the Free, answered:

'You have repented your attachment to imitative "teachers", but you have not yet repented your own self-esteem, which makes you imagine that you have a responsibility to the prisoners of the false. Many of the prisoners are themselves still caught in the web of deceit because they, too, have not repented deceit and want easy knowledge.'

'What should we do?' asked Emirudin Arosi.

'Come to me with an open heart and without conditions, even if such conditions are the service of mankind, or my appearing to you to be reasonable,' said the Master, 'for the release of your companions may be a matter for experts, not for you. Your capacity even to form an opinion about me is impaired, and I for one refuse to rely upon it.'

But, quite naturally, afraid that they might be making another mistake, Arosi and his wife passed on, to find another man: one who would comfort them. And they did. He, as it happened, was just another fraud.

Years again passed, and the couple made their way back to the house of Khwaja Ahrar.

'We have come, in all submission,' they informed the keeper of the gate, 'to place ourselves in the hands of the Lord of the Free, as if we were corpses in the hands of the washer of the dead.'

'Good people,' said the gatekeeper, 'your resolve seems excellent, and much like that of those whom the Lord of the Free would often accept as disciples. But there is no second chance for you in this life – for Khwaja Ahrar is dead.'

BAHAUDIN AND THE WANDERER

Bahaudin el-Shah, great teacher of the Naqshbandi dervishes, one day met a confrère in the great square of Bokhara.

The newcomer was a wandering Kalendar of the Malamati, the 'Blameworthy'. Bahaudin was surrounded by disciples.

'From where do you come?' he asked the traveller, in the usual Sufi phrase.

'I have no idea,' said the other, grinning foolishly.

Some of Bahaudin's disciples murmured their disapproval of this disrespect.

'Where are you going?' persisted Bahaudin.

'I do not know,' shouted the dervish.

'What is Good?' By now a large crowd had gathered.

'I do not know.'

'What is Evil?'

'I have no idea.'

'What is Right?'

'Whatever is good for me.'

'What is Wrong?'

'Whatever is bad for me.'

The crowd, irritated beyond its patience by this

dervish, drove him away. He went off, striding purposefully in a direction which led nowhere, as far as anyone knew.

'Fools!' said Bahaudin Naqshband, 'this man is acting the part of humanity. While you were despising him, he was deliberately demonstrating heedlessness as each of you does, all unaware, every day of your lives.'

FOOD AND PENS

Once upon a time – and this is a true story – there was a student. He used to go every day to sit at the feet of a Sufi teacher, to take down on paper what the master said.

Because he was so fully occupied with his studies, he was unable to follow any gainful occupation. One evening when he arrived home, his wife placed a bowl before him, covered with a napkin.

He took the cloth and put it around his neck, and then he saw that the dish was full of – pens and paper.

'Since this is what you do all day,' she said, 'just try to eat it.'

The next morning the student went, as usual, to learn from his teacher. Although his wife's words had distressed him, he continued to follow the accustomed pattern of studies, and did not go out looking for a job.

After a few minutes' writing, he found that his pen was not working well. 'Never mind,' said the master, 'go into that corner and bring the box you will find there and put it in front of you.'

When he sat down with the box and opened its lid, he found that it was full of – food.

THE GLANCE OF POWER

A dervish who had studied at the feet of a great Sufi teacher was told to perfect his knowledge of the sensing-exercise, and then to return to his master for further instruction. He retired to a forest and concentrated upon inner meditations with great force and application until hardly anything could disturb him.

He had, however, not concentrated well enough upon the need to keep all his objectives equally in his heart, and his zeal to succeed in his exercise proved somewhat stronger than his resolve to return to the school from which he had been sent to meditate.

Thus it was that, one day, while he was concentrating upon his inner self, a slight sound caught his ear. Annoyed at this, the dervish looked upwards into the branches of a tree from which the sound seemed to come, and saw a bird. The thought crossed his mind that this bird had no right to interrupt the exercises of so dedicated a man. No sooner had he conceived this idea than the bird dropped dead at his feet.

Now the dervish was not sufficiently advanced in the path of Sufihood to realise that there are tests all the way along the road. All that he could see at that moment was that he had attained a power such as he had never had before. HE could kill a living thing; or it might even be that the bird had been killed by some force other than one within himself, and all because it had interrupted his devotions!

'I must indeed be a great Sufi,' thought the dervish.

He got up and started to walk towards the nearest town.

When he got there, he saw an elegant house and decided to ask there for something to eat. When the door was opened by a woman at his knock, the dervish said:

'Woman, bring me food, for I am an advanced dervish, and there is merit in feeding those who are on the Path.'

'As soon as I can, revered Sage,' answered the lady, and she disappeared within.

But quite a long time passed, and still the woman did not come back. With each moment that passed, the dervish became more and more impatient. When the woman returned, he said to her:

'Consider yourself lucky that I do not direct upon you the wrath of the dervish, for does not everyone know that ill-fortune can come through disobedience of the Elect?'

'Ill-fortune can indeed come, unless one is unable to resist it through some experiences of one's own,' said the woman.

'How dare you answer me like that!' the dervish shouted, 'And what, in any case, do you mean?'

'I only mean,' said the woman, 'That I am not a bird in a forest clearing.'

At these words the dervish was astounded. 'My wrath is not harming you, and you can even read my thoughts,' he spluttered.

And he begged the woman to become his teacher.

'If you have disobeyed your own original teacher, you will fail me, too,' said the woman.

'Well, at least tell me how you reached a stage of understanding so much greater than mine,' asked the dervish.

'By obeying my teacher. He told me to attend his lectures and his exercises when he called me; otherwise I was to regard my worldly tasks as my exercises. In this way, though I have not heard from him for years, my inner life has constantly expanded, giving me such powers as you have seen, and many others.'

The dervish returned to the tekkia of his teacher for further guidance. The master refused to allow him to discuss anything, but merely said when he appeared:

'Go and serve under a certain scavenger who cleans the streets in such-and-such a town.'

Because the dervish held his teacher in such high regard, he went to that town. But when he arrived at the place where the scavenger worked, and saw him standing there covered in filth, he recoiled from approaching him and could not imagine himself as his servant.

As he stood there irresolutely, the scavenger said, calling him by his name:

'Lajaward, what bird would you kill today? Lajaward, what woman may read your thoughts today? Lajaward, what revolting duty will your teacher impose upon you tomorrow?'

Lajaward asked him:

'How can you see into my mind? How can a scavenger do things which pious hermits cannot do? Who are you?'

The scavenger said:

'Some pious hermits can do these things, but they do not do them for you because they have other things to do.

To you I look like a scavenger because that is my occupation. Because you do not like the work, you do not like the man. Because you imagine that holiness is washing and squatting and meditation, you will never find it. I have attained my present capacities because I never thought about holiness: I thought about duty. When people teach you duty to a master, or duty to something sacred, they are teaching you *duty*, you fool! All you can see is the "duty to man", or "duty to the temple". Because you cannot concentrate upon duty, you are as good as lost.'

And Lajaward, when he was able to forget that he was the servant of a scavenger, and realised that being a servant was a duty, became the man we know as the Enlightened, the Miracle-Working, the Rarely-Perfumed Sheikh Abdurrazaq Lajawardi of Badakhshan.

NOTHING FOR MAN EXCEPT
WHAT HE HAS EARNED

The superior experience and knowledge will be made available to a man or woman in exact accordance with his worth, capacity and earning of it. Hence, if a donkey sees a melon he will eat its rind; ants will eat whatever they can get hold of; man will consume without knowing that he has consumed.

Our objective is to achieve, by the understanding of the Origin, the Knowledge which comes through experience.

This is done, as with a journey, only with those who already know the Way.

The justice of this state is the greatest justice of all: because, while this knowledge cannot be withheld from him who deserves it, it cannot be given to him who does not deserve it.

It is the only substance with a discriminating faculty of its own, inherent justice.

(Yusuf Hamadani.)

MILK AND BUTTERMILK

Murid Laki Humayun put this question to the Maulana Bahaudin:

'In the town of Gulafshan there is a circle of followers. Some of them are in the condition of exercises, but the majority are those who collect weekly to learn from the daily transactions and teachings of the *murshid* (guide).

Many of the *murids* (disciples) understand the meaning of the tales and the events, and use these to correct their outward and inward behaviour.

Many of the outside followers, however, do not appear to benefit from the events and the transactions, seeking instead books and teachings which will give them precise promises of progress.

How is it that disciples are in pain when ordinary followers fail to understand the meaning of the stories and events, especially since many of the latter are their close friends and each desires that there should be a unification between disciples and followers even of the outward sort?'

Bahaudin replied:

'Discipleship was instituted in order to concentrate those who can learn without raw objectives. Disciples who grieve because their fellows are not learning in the same manner and at the same rate are grieving because they have imagined that affection must produce capacity. Capacity, however, is earned: affection is given and taken.

Accidental collections of people centring around a teaching will always endure a separating-out, like the separating of butter from milk, in the presence of the agitating factor, which is manifest or concealed but none the less present, whenever a renewal of teaching starts to work. This is the shaking of the vessel containing the milk. People imagine that, like buttermilk, when there is a movement (*jumbish*), they will all be affected in the same way. But both butter and skimmed milk have their functions, although these may be in different fields.'

THE TALISMAN

It is reported that a fakir who wanted to learn without effort was after a time turned away from the circle of Sheikh Shah Gwath Shattar. When Shattar was dismissing him, the Fakir said:

'You have the reputation of being able to teach all wisdom in the twinkling of an eye, yet you expect me to spend much time with you!'

'You have not yet learned to learn how to learn; but you will find out what I mean,' said the Sufi.

The Fakir pretended to go away, but he used to steal into the tekkia every night in order to see what the Sheikh did. Not long afterwards he saw Shah Gwath take a jewel out of a certain engraved metal casket. This gem he held over the heads of his disciples, saying: 'This is the repository of my knowledge, and it is none other than the Talisman of Illumination.'

'So this is the secret of the Sheikh's power,' thought the Fakir.

In the advanced hours of that very night, he entered the meditation-hall again and stole the talisman.

But in his hands the jewel, no matter how he tried,

33

would yield no power and no secrets. He was bitterly disappointed.

He set himself up as a teacher, enrolled disciples and tried again and again to illuminate them, or himself, by means of the talisman, but all to no avail.

One day he was sitting in his shrine, after his disciples had gone to bed, meditating upon his problems, when Shattar appeared before him.

'O Fakir!' said Shah Gwath, 'you can always steal something, but you cannot always make it work. You can even steal knowledge, but it can be useless to you, like the thief who stole the barber's razor, made through the knowledge of the swordsmith but lacking the knowledge of shaving. He set himself up as a barber and died in misery when he could not even shave a single beard, but instead cut several throats.'

'But I have the talisman, and you have not,' said the Fakir.

'Yes, *you* have the talisman, but *I* am Shattar,' said the Sufi. 'I can, with my skill, make another talisman. You, with the talisman, cannot become Shattar.'

'Why, then, have you come – merely to torture me?' cried the Fakir.

'I came to tell you that, if you had not been so literal-minded as to imagine that to have a thing is the same as being capable of being transformed by it, you would have been ready to learn how to learn.'

But the Fakir thought that the Sufi was only trying to get his talisman back, and, because he was not ready to learn how to learn, he decided to persist in experiments with the jewel.

His disciples continued to do so: and their followers, and theirs. In fact, the rituals which are the result of his

34

restless experimenting nowadays form the essence of their religion. Nobody could imagine, so sanctified by time have these observances become, that they had their origin in the circumstances which have just been related.

The hoary practitioners of the faith, too, are held to be so venerable and infallible, that these beliefs will never die.

DISPUTE WITH ACADEMICS

It is recorded that Bahaudin Naqshband was asked:

'Why do you not dispute with scholastics? Such-and-such a sage regularly does so. This causes the scholars' total confusion, and his own disciples' invariable admiration.'

He said: 'Go and ask those who remember the time when I myself used to contend with academics. I regularly refuted their surmises and their imagined proofs with relative ease. Those who were then present on numerous occasions will tell you that. But, one day, a wiser man than I said:

' "You so frequently and predictably shame the men of the tongue that there is a monotony in it. This is especially so because it is to no final purpose, since the academicians are without understanding, and continue to wrangle long after their positions have been demolished." He added: "Your students are in a constant state of wonderment at your victories. They have learned to admire you. Instead they should have perceived the comparative worthlessness and lack of significance of your opponents. You have thus, in victory, failed by, let us say, a quarter.

37

' "Their wonderment, too, takes up much of their time, when they could be appreciating something worthwhile. So you have failed by perhaps another quarter. Two quarters are equal to one-half. You have one-half of an opportunity left."

'That was twenty years ago. That is why I do not trouble myself or others with scholars, whether for victory or defeat.

'Now and again one may strike the self-appointed scholars a blow, to demonstrate their hollowness to students: as one hits an empty pot. To do any more is both wasteful and tantamount to giving intellectuals an importance, through granting them gratuitous attention, that they certainly could not attain by themselves.'

THE STORY OF HIRAVI

At the time of King Mahmud the Conqueror of Ghazna there lived a young man by the name of Haidar Ali Jan. His father, Iskandar Khan, decided to obtain for him the patronage of the Emperor, and he sent him to study spiritual matters under the greatest sages of the time.

Haidar Ali, when he had mastered the repetitions and the exercises, when he knew the recitals and the bodily postures of the Sufi schools, was taken by his father into the presence of the Emperor.

'Mighty Mahmud,' said Iskandar, 'I have had this youth, my eldest and most intelligent son, specially trained in the ways of the Sufis, so that he might obtain a worthy position at your Majesty's court, knowing that you are the patron of learning of our epoch.'

Mahmud did not look up, but he merely said: 'Bring him back in a year.'

Slightly disappointed, but nursing high hopes, Iskandar sent Ali to study the works of the great Sufis of the past, and to visit the shrines of the ancient masters in Baghdad, so that the intervening time would not be wasted.

When he brought the youth back to the court, he said:

39

'Peacock of the Age! My son has carried out long and difficult journeys, and at the same time to his knowledge of exercises he has added a complete familiarity with the classics of the People of the Path. Pray have him examined, so that it may be shown that he could be an adornment of your Majesty's court.'

'Let him,' said Mahmud immediately, 'return after another year.'

During the next twelve months Haidar Ali crossed the Oxus and visited Bokhara and Samarkand, Qasr-i-Arifin and Tashqand, Dushambe and the turbats of the Sufi saints of Turkestan.

When he returned to the court, Mahmud of Ghazna took one look at him and said:

'He may care to come back after a further year.'

Haidar Ali made the pilgrimage to Mecca in that year. He travelled to India; and in Persia he consulted rare books and never missed an opportunity of seeking out and paying his respects to the great dervishes of the time.

When he returned to Ghazna, Mahmud said to him:

'Now select a teacher, if he will have you, and come back in a year.'

When that year was over and Iskandar Khan prepared to take his son to the court, Haidar Ali showed no interest at all in going there. He simply sat at the feet of his teacher in Herat, and nothing that his father could say would move him.

'I have wasted my time, and my money, and this young man has failed the tests imposed by Mahmud the King,' he lamented, and he abandoned the whole affair.

Meanwhile the day when the youth was due to present himself came and went, and then Mahmud said to his courtiers:

'Prepare yourselves for a visit to Herat, there is someone there whom I have to see.'

As the Emperor's cavalcade was entering Herat to the
flourish of trumpets, Haidar Ali's teacher took him by
the hand. He led him to the gate of the tekkia, and
there they waited.

Shortly afterwards Mahmud and his courtier Ayaz,
taking off their shoes, presented themselves at the
sanctuary.

'Here, Mahmud,' said the Sufi sheikh, 'is the man who
was nothing while he was a visitor of kings; but who is
now one who is visited by kings. Take him as your Sufi
counsellor: for he is ready.'

This is the story of the studies of Hiravi, Haidar Ali
Jan, the Sage of Herat.

SOMETHING TO LEARN FROM MIRI

The renowned Sufi sage Baba Saifdar had a disciple named Miri, who used to complain that Saifdar hardly ever saw him after he had been admitted into discipleship.

'I was better off before he made me a pupil,' he would say, 'because then I was treated at least as a friend and could benefit from his companionship.'

Baba Saifdar, however, knew the inner condition of his student, but made no reference to it on their rare meetings. He preferred to await the chance to provide an effective demonstration of the relationship and its meaning.

One day Miri was giving evidence at an open-air court when Baba Saifdar passed.

The judge had just said to the witness:

'Do you positively remember having seen the accused at the robbery?'

Miri, catching sight of his teacher and recalling as a consequence only the 'remembering' exercise which he had learned from him, called out involuntarily, 'I remember!'

The alleged thief was immediately convicted on this 'eye-witness' statement. He was innocent; and when Miri retracted his identification, he was nearly tried for perjury.

When he was eventually released, the Baba said to him:

'That was a parallel, in ordinary matters, with what can happen in more profound affairs. Praise and complaint of one's teachers leads to folly. So does any disregard for their rules. What is visible to them is invisible to the student.'

'I can only hope that my example may be of value to others, so that, far from having inevitably to go through this sort of experience, they may be enabled to proceed to higher things,' said Miri.

This story is for that reason called 'Miri's Lesson'.

THE MAD KING'S IDOL

There was once a violent, ignorant and idolatrous king. One day he swore that if his personal idol accorded him a certain advantage in life, he would capture the first three people who passed by his castle, and force them to dedicate themselves to idol-worship.

Sure enough, the king's wish was fulfilled, and he immediately sent soldiers on to the highway to bring in the first three people whom they could find.

These three were, as it happened, a scholar, a Sayed (descendant of Mohammed the Prophet) and a prostitute.

Having them thrown down before his idol, the unbalanced king told them of his vow, and ordered them all to bow down in front of the image.

The scholar said:

'This situation undoubtedly comes within the doctrine of "force majeure". There are numerous precedents allowing anyone to appear to conform with custom if compelled, without real legal or moral culpability being in any way involved.'

So he made a deep obeisance to the idol.

The Sayed, when it was his turn, said:

'As a specially protected person, having in my veins

the blood of the Holy Prophet, my actions themselves purify anything which is done, and therefore there is no bar to my acting as this man demands.'

And he bowed down before the idol.

The prostitute said:

'Alas, I have neither intellectual training nor special prerogatives, and so I am afraid that, whatever you do to me, I cannot worship this idol, even in appearance.'

The mad king's malady was immediately banished by this remark. As if by magic he saw the deceit of the two worshippers of the image. He at once had the scholar and the Sayed decapitated, and set the prostitute free.

TWO SIDES

Part-coloured dervish robes, since copied for teaching purposes and eventually imitated for sheer decoration, were introduced into Spain, in the Middle Ages, in this manner:

A Frankish king had a taste for pageantry, and he also prided himself on his grasp of philosophy. He asked a Sufi known as 'The Agarin' to instruct him in the High Wisdom. The Agarin said:

'We offer you observation and reflection, but first you must learn their extension.'

'We already know how to extend our attention, having studied well all the preliminary steps to wisdom from our own tradition,' said the king.

'Very well,' said the Agarin, 'we shall give your Majesty a demonstration of our teaching at a pageant tomorrow.'

Arrangements were duly made, and the next day the dervishes of the Agarin's *ribat* (teaching centre) filed through the narrow streets of that Andalusian town. The king and his courtiers were assembled on either side of the route: grandees on the right and men-at-arms on the left.

When the procession was over, the Agarin turned to the king and said:

'Majesty, please ask your knights, from opposite, the colours of the dervish robes.'

The knights all swore on the scriptures and upon their honour that the costumes had been blue.

The king and the rest of the Court were amazed and confused, for this was not what they had seen at all. 'We all distinctly saw that they were dressed in *brown* habits,' said the king, 'and among us are men of great sanctity in faith and well respected.'

He ordered all his knights to be prepared for punishment and degradation.

Those who saw the clothes as brown were sent to one side to be rewarded.

These proceedings lasted for some time. Afterwards the king said to the Agarin:

'What bewitchment have you performed, evil man? What devilment is this which can cause the most honourable knights in Christendom to defy truth, abandon their hope of redemption and betray indications of unreliability which render them useless for battle?'

The Sufi said:

'The half of the robes visible on your side was brown. The other half of each robe was blue. Without preparation, your expectancy causes you to deceive yourself about us. How can we teach anyone anything under such circumstances?'

WELCOMES

We welcome the scholars who want to understand the Path.

What of the others? They think that we do not welcome them, but it is in reality they who do not welcome us.

They cannot do so while they retain such strange conceptions of the Way.

I refer to two kinds: those who say: 'We deny the value of Sufism,' and those who say: 'We accept Sufism, but this is not it.'

Of the two, those who reject the Sufis are better than those who pretend that the people whom they do not like cannot therefore be Sufis.

The former class are deluded by others into believing that Sufis are useless: and anyone may be deceived by others.

And the latter class are those who are deluded by themselves into imagining something which is not correct.

No scholar can decide who is or who is not a Sufi. People trying to do something of which they are incapable should always be a lesson to us.

AJMAL HUSSEIN AND THE SCHOLARS

Sufi Ajmal Hussein was constantly being criticised by scholars, who feared that his repute might outshine their own. They spared no efforts to cast doubts upon his knowledge, to accuse him of taking refuge from their criticisms in mysticism, and even to imply that he had been guilty of discreditable practices.

At length he said:

'If I answer my critics, they make it the opportunity to bring fresh accusation against me, which people believe because it amuses them to believe such things. If I do not answer them they crow and preen themselves, and people believe that they are real scholars. They imagine that we Sufis oppose scholarship. We do not. But our very existence is a threat to the pretended scholarship of tiny noisy ones. Scholarship long since disappeared. What we have to face now is sham scholarship.'

The scholars shrilled more loudly than ever. At last Ajmal said:

'Argument is not as effective as demonstration. I shall give you an insight into what these people are like.'

He invited 'question papers' from the scholars, to allow them to test his knowledge and ideas. Fifty different professors and academicians sent questionnaires to him. Ajmal answered them all differently. When the scholars met to discuss these papers, at a conference, there were so many versions of what he believed, that each one thought that he had exposed Ajmal, and refused to give up his thesis in favour of any other. The result was the celebrated 'brawling of the scholars'. For five days they attacked each other bitterly.

'This,' said Ajmal, 'is a demonstration. What matters to each one most is his own opinion and his own interpretation. They care nothing for truth. This is what they do with everyone's teachings. When he is alive, they torment him. When he dies they become experts on his works. The real motive of the activity, however, is to vie with one another and to oppose anyone outside their own ranks. Do you want to become one of them? Make a choice soon.'

TIMUR AND HAFIZ

The Sufi poet Hafiz of Shiraz wrote the famous poem:

> If that Sharazi Turkish maid would take my heart
> Into her hand:
> I'd give Bokhara for the mole upon her cheek—
> Or Samarkand.

The conqueror Tamerlane had Hafiz brought before him and said:

'How can you give away Bokhara and Samarkand for a woman? Besides, they are in my own domains, and I shall not permit anyone to pretend that they are not!'

Hafiz said to him:

'Your meanness may have given you power. My generosity has put me in your power. Your meanness is obviously more effective than my prodigality.'

Tamerlane laughed and let the Sufi go.

FULL UP

A man came to Bahaudin Naqshband, and said:

'I have travelled from one teacher to another, and I have studied many Paths, all of which have given me great benefits and many advantages of all kinds.

'I now wish to be enrolled as one of your disciples, so that I may drink from the well of knowledge, and thus make myself more and more advanced in the Tariqa, the Mystic Way.'

Bahaudin, instead of answering the question directly, called for dinner to be served. When the dish of rice and meat stew was brought, he pressed plateful after plateful upon his guest. Then he gave him fruits and pastries, and then he called for more *pilau*, and more and more courses of food, vegetables, salads, confitures.

At first the man was flattered, and as Bahaudin showed pleasure at every mouthful he swallowed, he ate as much as he could. When his eating slowed down, the Sufi Sheikh seemed very annoyed, and to avoid his displeasure, the unfortunate man ate virtually another meal.

When he could not swallow even another grain of rice, and rolled in great discomfort upon a cushion, Bahaudin addressed him in this manner:

'When you came to see me, you were as full of undigested teachings as you now are with meat, rice and fruit. You felt discomfort, and, because you are unaccustomed to spiritual discomfort of the real kind, you interpreted this as a hunger for more knowledge. Indigestion was your real condition.

'I can teach you if you will now follow my instructions and stay here with me digesting by means of activities which will not seem to you to be initiatory, but which will be equal to the eating of something which will enable your meal to be digested and transformed into nutrition, not weight.'

The man agreed. He told his story many decades later, when he became famous as the great teacher Sufi Khalii Ashrafzada.

CHARKHI AND HIS UNCLE

It is related that a young disciple of Baba Charkhi was sitting in the hallway of his house when a man arrived and said: 'Who are you?'

The disciple answered: 'I am a follower of Baba Charkhi.'

The man said: 'How can Charkhi have followers? I am his uncle, and I would have known if he had. As to his being a "Baba", you have been misinformed, my child.'

Charkhi's uncle stayed in the house after that for many years, until he died. He refused to enter the 'assemblies of culture' held by the Baba, and he could never credit that Charkhi was a Sufi teacher. 'I have known him since he was a child,' he said, 'and I cannot see him teaching anything, because he was never able to learn anything.'

Even after Charkhi died, there were many people, some of them frequent visitors to his house, including merchants with whom he had business dealings, who did not believe that he was a saint.

Yunus Abu-Aswad Kamali, the theologian, spoke for some of these when he said: 'I knew Charkhi for thirty years, and he never discussed higher things with me. To my mind, such behaviour is impossible to a learned man. He never tried to describe his theories, and he did not attempt to make me a disciple. I only heard of his supposedly being a Sufi through the butcher.'

THE PRISONER OF SAMARKAND

Hakim Iskandar Zaramez and Abdulwahab el Hindi were passing the corner of a large house in Samarkand one day when they heard a wild cry.

'They are torturing some poor wretch,' said El Hindi, stopping and standing still as the cries increased.

'Would you have the suffering eased?' asked Zaramez.

'Naturally. As a Wali, a saint, you can surely do it, if there be God's permission.'

'Very well,' said the Hakim, 'and I shall demonstrate something.'

Zaramez moved five paces away from the corner of the house. The cries stopped.

'You withdraw, and the tumult ceases! Assuredly I have always heard that it is the nearness to an afflicted person which assuages pain,' said El Hindi.

The Hakim smiled, but said no more, making the sign which among the Sufis signifies: 'A question may have no answer at a certain time because of the state of the querent'.

Many years later when El Hindi was in Morocco, he listened to a dervish relating his experiences to a group of students one night in the closed city of Maula Idriss.

Among other things, the dervish said:

'On such-and-such a day of the month of Ramadan el-Mubarak, so many years ago, I was seized as a vagrant because of my apparent poverty and meagre appearance. I was left in a stone-built cell at one corner of the outside wall of the Kazi's house, pending judgment. This was in the northern vicinity of Samarkand.

'I had been contented enough with my lot, and sitting in silent contemplation when I felt, quite unmistakably and from outside, not far away, the presence of a saint. I started to howl and shriek, and to throw myself about; because a power was upon me, and because I could not escape however much I wanted to approach him.

'Then I felt that he had moved away as if disturbed by my clamour. I tried to let him come near again by letting myself become as slack and silent as the night.'

The sheikh of the dervish circle said:

'Your experience could have instructed you that people are most profoundly affected by *baraka* (spiritual power) when for all apparent purposes it is beyond their reach. The Wali was teaching you this, even though you were in prison and he may have seemed to outside observers to be doing something entirely different, or even nothing at all.'

El Hindi relates:

'This occasion was the beginning of my real understanding that it is not wonderful that people have "spiritual experiences". What might be wonderful is that so few people have them. What is certainly more wonderful is that instead of learning from them, they worship the experience and count it as something which it is not.'

THE BOOK IN TURKI

A would-be disciple went to Bahaudin.

The master was surrounded by thirty of his students, in a garden, after dinner.

The newcomer said:

'I wish to serve you.'

Bahaudin answered:

'You can best serve me by reading my *Risalat* (Letters).'

'I have already done so,' said the newcomer.

'If you had done so in reality and not in appearance, you would not have approached me in this manner,' said Bahaudin.

He continued:

'Why do you think that you are able to learn?'

'I am ready to study with you.'

Bahaudin said:

'Let the most junior Murid (disciple) stand up.'

Anwari, who was sixteen years of age, rose to his feet.

'How long have you been with us?' asked El-Shah.

'Three weeks, O Murshid.'

'Have I taught you anything?'

'I do not know.'

'Do you think so?'

'I do not think so.'

Bahaudin said to him:

'In this newcomer's satchel you will find a book of poems. Take it in your hand and recite the entire contents without mistake and without even opening it.'

Awari found the book. He did not open it, but said: 'I fear that it is in Turki.'

Bahaudin said:

'Recite it!'

Anwari did so, and as he finished the stranger became more and more affected by this wonder – a book being read without being opened by some one who did not know Turki.

Falling at the feet of Bahaudin, he begged to be admitted to the Circle.

Bahaudin said:

'It is this kind of phenomenon which attracts you – while it still does, you cannot really benefit from it. That is why, even if you have read my *Risalat*, you have not really read it.'

'Come back,' he continued, 'when you have read it as this beardless boy has read it. It was only such study that gave him the power to recite from a book which he had not opened, and at the same time prevented him from grovelling in wonderment at the event.'

BEGGARS AND WORKERS

It is related of Ibn el-Arabi that people said to him:

'Your circle is composed mainly of beggars, husband-men and artizans. Can you not find people of intellect who will follow you, so that perhaps more authoritative notice might be taken of your teachings?'

He said:

'The Day of Calamity will be infinitely nearer when I have influential men and scholars singing my praises; for without any doubt they will be doing so for their own sake and not for the sake of our work!'

UNALTERED

Nawab Mohammed Khan, Jan-Fishan, was out walking in Delhi one day when he came upon a number of people seemingly engaged in an altercation.

He asked a bystander:

'What is happening here?'

The man said: 'Sublime Highness, one of your disciples is objecting to the behaviour of the people in this quarter.'

Jan-Fishan went into the crowd and said to his follower:

'Explain yourself.'

The man said: 'These people have been hostile.'

The people exclaimed: 'That is not true: we were, on the contrary, doing him honour for your sake.'

'What did they say?' asked the Nawab.

'They said: "Hail, Great Scholar!" I was telling them that it is the ignorance of scholars which is often responsible for the confusion and desperation of man.'

Jan-Fishan Khan said: 'It is the conceit of scholars which is responsible, quite often, for the misery of man. And it is *your* conceit in claiming to be other than a scholar which is the cause of this tumult. Not to be a scholar, which involves detachment from the petty, is an accomplishment. Scholars are seldom wise, being only un-altered people stuffed with thoughts and books.

'These people were trying to honour you. If some people think that mud is gold, if it is their mud, respect it. You are not their teacher.

'Do you not realise that, in behaving in such a sensitive and self-willed manner, you are acting just like a scholar, and therefore deserve the name, even if it is an epithet?

'Guard yourself, my child. Too many slips from the Path of Supreme Attainment – and you may become a scholar.'

DIAGNOSIS

Bahaudin Naqshband once visited the town of Alucha, after a deputation of citizens, hearing that he was passing along the nearby highway, waited upon him and begged him to spend some time with them.

'Do you want to satisfy your curiosity about me, to entertain me and do me honour, or to invite me to impart my teachings to you?' he asked them.

The leader of the party, after a consultation with his fellows, replied:

'We have heard much of you, and you can have heard nothing of us. Since you apparently give us the rare privilege of receiving your teaching, we will gratefully accept this from the alternatives which you have offered.'

Bahaudin entered the town.

The whole populace assembled in the public square. Their own spiritual teachers ushered Bahaudin to a place of honour, and when he was seated, the chief of the philosophers of Alucha began to address him in these terms:

'Sublime Presence and Great Teacher! We have all heard of you, for who has not? But, since you are doubtless unfamiliar with the thoughts of such insignificant people as ourselves, we beg to be allowed to delineate our ideas to you, so that you may support, amend or refute them for us, to our certain profit . . .'

But Bahaudin stopped them, saying:

'I will certainly tell you what you can do, but you need not tell me anything about yourselves.'

He then proceeded to describe to the people their methods of thought and also their own shortcomings and the precise manner in which they looked upon different problems of life and of man.

After this, he said to the astonished citizens:

'Now, before I tell you how you may remedy this state of affairs, perhaps you will voice any feelings suppressed in your hearts, in order that I might explain myself for your edification, so that you could attend more completely to what I am about to say.'

The same spokesman, after conferring with the people, said:

'O ancient and guide! The unanimous cause of our wonderment and curiosity is how you could know so much about us and our problems and our speculations. Are we right in inferring that such knowledge can only exist where there is a superior form of direct perception, in an unusually blessed individual?'

In answer, Bahaudin called for a jug, some water in a pitcher, some salt and flour. He poured salt, flour and water into the jug. Then he said to the chief spokesman:

'Please be good enough to tell me what is in this jug.'

The man said:

'Reverence, there is a mixture of flour, water and salt.'

'How do you know the composition of the mixture?' asked Bahaudin.

'When the ingredients are known,' said the spokesman,

'there can be no doubt about the nature of the mixture.'

'That is the answer to your question, which surely requires no further explanation from me,' said Bahaudin Naqshband.

THE KASHKUL

It is related that a dervish once stopped a king in the street. The king said: 'How dare you, a man of no account, interrupt the progress of your sovereign?'

The dervish answered:

'Can you be a sovereign if you cannot even fill my kashkul, the begging-bowl?'

He held out his bowl, and the king ordered it to be filled with gold.

But, no sooner was the bowl seen to be full of coins than they disappeared, and the bowl seemed to be empty again.

Sack after sack of gold was brought, and still the amazing bowl devoured coins.

'Stop!' shouted the king, 'for this trickster is emptying my treasury!'

'To you I am emptying your treasury,' said the dervish, 'but to others I am merely illustrating a truth.'

'And the truth?' asked the king.

'The truth is that, the bowl is the desires of man, and the gold what man is given. There is no end to man's capacity to devour, without being in any way changed. See, the bowl has eaten nearly all your wealth, but it is still a carved sea-coconut, and has not partaken of the nature of gold in any respect.

'If you care,' continued the dervish, 'to step into this bowl, it will devour you, too. How can a king, then, hold himself as being of any account?'

THE COW

Once upon a time there was a cow. In all the world there was no animal which so regularly gave so much milk of such high quality.

People came from far and wide to see this wonder. The cow was extolled by all. Fathers told their children of its dedication to its appointed task. Ministers of religion adjured their flocks to emulate it in their own way. Government officials referred to it as a paragon which right behaviour, planning and thinking could duplicate in the human community. Everyone was, in short, able to benefit from the existence of this wonderful animal.

There was, however, one feature which most people, absorbed as they were by the obvious advantages of the cow, failed to observe. It had a little habit, you see. And this habit was that, as soon as a pail had been filled with its admittedly unparalleled milk – it kicked it over.

INDIVIDUALITY AND QUALITY

Yaqub, the son of the Judge, said that one day he questioned Bahaudin Naqshband in this manner:

'When I was in companionship with the Murshid of Tabriz, he regularly made a sign that he was not to be spoken to, when he was in a condition of special reflection. But you are accessible to us at all times. Am I correct in concluding that this difference is due to your undoubtedly greater capacity of detachment, the capacity being under your dominion, rather than fugitive?'

Bahaudin told him:

'No, you are always seeking comparisons between people and between states. You are always seeking evidences and differences, when you are not you are seeking similarities. You do not really need so much explanation in matters which are outside such measurement. Different modes of behaviour on the part of the wise are to be regarded as due to differences in individuality, not of quality.'

PARADISE OF SONG

Ahangar was a mighty swordsmith who lived in one of Afghanistan's remote eastern valleys. In time of peace he made steel ploughs, shoed horses and, above all, he sang.

The songs of Ahangar, who is known by different names in various parts of Central Asia, were eagerly listened to by the people of the valleys. They came from the forests of giant walnut-trees, from the snowcapped Hindu-Kush, from Qataghan and Badakhshan, from Khanabad and Kunar, from Herat and Paghman, to hear his songs.

Above all, the people came to hear the song of all songs, which was Ahangar's Song of the Valley of Paradise.

This song had a haunting quality, and a strange lilt, and most of all it had a story which was so strange that people felt they knew the remote Valley of Paradise of which the smith sang. Often they asked him to sing it when he was not in the mood to do so, and he would refuse. Sometimes people asked him whether the Valley was truly real, and Ahangar could only say:

'The Valley of the Song is as real as real can be.'

77

'But how do you know?' the people would ask, 'Have you ever been there?'

'Not in any ordinary way,' said Ahangar.

To Ahangar, and to nearly all the people who heard him, the Valley of the Song was, however, real, real as real can be.

Aisha, a local maiden whom he loved, doubted whether there was such a place. So, too, did Hasan, a braggart and fearsome swordsman who swore to marry Aisha, and who lost no opportunity of laughing at the smith.

One day, when the villagers were sitting around silently after Ahangar had been telling his tale to them, Hasan spoke:

'If you believe that this valley is so real, and that it is, as you say, in those mountains of Sangan yonder, where the blue haze rises, why do you not try to find it?'

'It would not be right, I know that,' said Ahangar.

'You know what it is convenient to know, and do not know what you do not want to know!' shouted Hasan. 'Now, my friend, I propose a test. You love Aisha, but she does not trust you. She has no faith in this absurd Valley of yours. You could never marry her, because when there is no confidence between man and wife, they are not happy and all manner of evils result.'

'Do you expect me to go to the valley, then?' asked Ahangar.

'Yes,' said Hasan and all the audience together.

'If I go and return safely, will Aisha consent to marry me?' asked Ahangar.

'Yes,' murmured Aisha.

So Ahangar, collecting some dried mulberries and a scrap of bread, set off for the distant mountains.

He climbed and climbed, until he came to a wall which encircled the entire range. When he had ascended its sheer sides, there was another wall, even more precipitous than the first. After that there was a third, then a fourth, and finally a fifth wall.

Descending on the other side, Ahangar found that he was in a valley, strikingly similar to his own.

People came out to welcome him, and as he saw them, Ahangar realised that something very strange was happening.

Months later, Ahangar the Smith, walking like an old man, limped into his native village, and made for his humble hut. As word of his return spread throughout the countryside, people gathered in front of his home to hear what his adventures had been.

Hasan the swordsman spoke for them all, and called Ahangar to his window.

There was a gasp as everyone saw how old he had become.

'Well, Master Ahangar, and did you reach the Valley of Paradise?'

'I did.'

'And what was it like?'

Ahangar, fumbling for his words, looked at the assembled people with a weariness and hopelessness that he had never felt before. He said:

'I climbed and I climbed, and I climbed. When it seemed as though there could be no human habitation in such a desolate place, and after many trials and disappointments. I came upon a valley. This valley was exactly like the one in which we live. And then I saw the people. Those people are not only like us people: they are *the same people*. For every Hasan, every Aisha, every Ahangar,

79

every anybody whom we have here, there is another one, exactly the same in that valley.

'These are likenesses and reflections to us, when we see such things. But it is we who are the likeness and reflection of them – we who are here, we are their twins . . .'

Everyone thought that Ahangar had gone mad through his privations, and Aisha married Hasan the swordsman. Ahangar rapidly grew old and died. And all the people, every one who had heard this story from the lips of Ahangar, first lost heart in their lives, then grew old and died, for they felt that something was going to happen over which they had no control and from which they had no hope, and so they lost interest in life itself.

It is only once in a thousand years that this secret is seen by man. When he sees it, he is changed. When he tells its bare facts to others, they wither and die out.

People think that such an event is a catastrophe, and so they must not know about it, for they cannot understand (such is the nature of their ordinary life) that they have more selves than one, more hopes than one, more chances than one – up there, in the Paradise of the Song of Ahangar the mighty smith.

THE TREASURE OF THE CUSTODIANS

A prince of the illustrious House of Abbas, kinsfolk of the Prophet's uncle, was living a humble life in Mosul of Iraq. His family had fallen upon evil times, and had reverted to the common lot of man to labour. After three generations the family was somewhat restored, and the prince had the status of a small shopkeeper.

As is the custom with the noble among the Arabs, this man, whose name was Daud el Abbassi, merely called himself Daud, son of Altaf. He spent his days in the marketplace, selling beans and herbs, trying to repair the family's fortunes.

This process continued for some years until Daud fell in love with the daughter of a rich merchant: Zobeida Ibnat Tawil. She was more than willing to marry him, but there was a custom in her family that any prospective son-in-law would have to match a rare gem specially selected by the father, in order to prove his resourcefulness and also his material worth.

After the preliminary negotiations, when Daud was shown the glittering ruby which Tawil had chosen for the test to win his daughter, the young shopkeeper's heart became heavy. Not only was this gem of the finest water, but its size and colour were such that the mines of Badakhsan could surely never have yielded anything of that kind more than once in a thousand years...

Time passed, and Daud thought of every means he could to find the money which he would need even to try to match the jewel. He at length discovered from a jeweller that he had but one chance. If he sent out criers to offer anyone producing its equal not only his house and all his possessions, but also three-quarters of every penny which he would earn for the rest of his natural life, there might be a chance to find a similar ruby.

Accordingly, Daud caused this announcement to be made.

Day after day the word went forth that a ruby of astonishing value, brilliance and colour was being sought, and people from far and near hastened to the house of the merchant to see whether they could provide anything so magnificent. But, after a lapse of almost three years, Daud found that there was no ruby in Arabistan or Ajam, in Khorasan or Hind, in Africa or the West, in Java or Ceylon, which came anything near the excellence of the one which his prospective father-in-law had found.

Zobeida and Daud were at the point of despair. It seemed as though they were never to marry, for the girl's father refused adamantly to accept anything less than a perfect match for his ruby.

One evening, when Daud was sitting in his small garden trying to think, for the thousanth time, of some means to win Zobeida, he realised that a tall and emaciated figure was standing beside him. In his hand he had a staff, on his head was a dervish cap; slung at his waist was a metal begging bowl.

'Peace upon you, O my king!' said Daud in the customary salutation, rising to his feet.

'Daud, the Abbassi, scion of the House of Koreish!' said the apparition, 'I am one of the guardians of the treasures of the Apostle, and I have come to help you in your extremity. You seek a matchless ruby. I shall give it to you, from the treasures of your patrimony, left safe in the hands of the penniless custodians!'

Daud looked at him and said: 'All the treasure which was in the possession of our House was spent, sold, plundered centuries ago. We have nothing left but our name, and we do not even use that for fear of dishonouring it. How can there be any treasure left out of my patrimony?'

'There can still be treasure, precisely because it was not all left in the hands of the House,' said the dervish; 'for people always first rob those who are known to have something to steal. When, however, that is gone, thieves do not then know where to look. This is the first measure of security of the Custodians.'

Daud reflected that many dervishes are reputed to be eccentrics and so he only said:

'Who would leave priceless treasures such as a gem like Tawil's in the hands of a ragged beggar? And what tattered beggar, having been given even one such thing, would forebear from throwing it away, or selling it and spending the proceeds in an insane bout of reckless-ness?'

The dervish answered:

'My son, this is exactly what people are expected to think. Because beggars are ragged, people imagine that they desire clothes. Because a man has a jewel, people imagine that he will throw it away if he is not a thrifty merchant. Your thoughts are the things which help to make our treasure secure.'

'Then take me to the treasure,' said Daud, 'so that I may end my intolerable doubts and fears.'

The dervish blindfolded Daud and made him ride, dressed as a blind man, for several days and nights on a mean donkey. They dismounted and walked through a mountain cleft, and when the cloth was removed from his eyes, Daud saw that he was standing in a treasure-house where incalculable quantities and unbelievable varieties of precious stones glittered from shelves in serried walls of stone.

'Can this be the treasure of my forefathers? Because I have never so much as heard of anything like it, even from the time of Haroun el-Raschid,' said Daud.

'You may be sure that it is,' said the dervish, 'and more than that: this is only the cavern which contains the jewels from which you may choose. There is much more.'

'And it is mine?'

'It is yours.'

'Then I will take it all,' said Daud, who was almost overcome by greed at the sight.

'You will take just what you have come here to take,' said the dervish, 'for you are as little fitted for the proper administration of this wealth as were your forebears. If this were not so, the Custodians would have handed back the entire treasure centuries ago.'

Daud chose the only ruby which exactly matched Tawil's, and the dervish bore him back to his house in the same way as he had brought him. Daud and Zobeida were married.

And in this way, it is related, the treasures of the House

are handed out to their proper inheritors whenever they
have real need for them. Today the Custodians are not
always patched dervishes in appearance. Sometimes they
are to all outward appearances the most ordinary of men.
But they will not yield the treasures except when there is
a real need.

THE ATTACHMENT CALLED GRACE

A studious and dedicated seeker after truth arrived at
the tekkia of Bahaudin Naqshband.

In accordance with custom, he attended the lectures
and asked no questions.

When Bahaudin at last said to him: 'Ask something of
me,' this man said:

'Shah, before I came to you I studied such-and-such a
philosophy under so-and-so. Attracted by your repute I
journeyed to your tekkia.

'Hearing your addresses I have been impressed by what
you are saying, and wish to continue my studies with
you.

'But, since I have such gratitude and attachment to my
former studies and teacher, I would like you either to
explain their connection with your work, or else to make
me forget them, so that I may continue without a divided
mind.'

Bahaudin said:

'I can do neither of these things. What I *can* do, however, is to inform you that one of the surest signs of human
vanity is to be attached to a person, and to a creed, and
to imagine that such attachment comes from a higher

source. If a man becomes obsessed by sweetmeats, he would call them divine, if anyone would allow it.

'With this information you can learn wisdom. Without it, you can only learn attachment and call it grace.'

'The man who needs *malumat* (information)

Always supposes that he needs *maarifat* (wisdom)

If he is really even a man of information, he will see that he next needs wisdom.

If he is a man of wisdom, he only then is free from the need for information.'

CORRECTION

Abdullah ben Yahya was showing a manuscript, which he had written, to a visitor.

This man said: 'But this word has been incorrectly spelt.'

He at once deleted the word and wrote it in the manner of which his guest approved.

When the man had left, Abdullah was asked: 'Why did you do that, considering that the "correction" was in fact inaccurate, and you wrote the wrong word where the original one had been right?'

He answered: 'That was a social occasion. The man thought he was helping me, and thought that the expression of his ignorance was an indication of knowledge. I applied the behaviour of culture and politeness, not the behaviour of truth, because when people want politeness and social interchange, they cannot stand truth. Had I stood in relation to this man as teacher to student, matters would have been different. Only stupid people and pedants imagine that their duty is to instruct everyone, when the motive of the people is generally not to seek instruction, but to attract attention.'

THE SAINT AND THE SINNER

There was once a dervish devotee who believed that it was his task to reproach those who did evil things and to enjoin upon them spiritual thoughts, so that they might find the right path. What this dervish did not know, however, was that a teacher is not only one who tells others to do things by acting through fixed principles. Unless the teacher knows exactly what the inner situation is, with each student, the teacher may suffer the reverse of what he desires.

However, this devotee one day found a man who gambled excessively, and did not know how to cure the habit. The dervish took up his position outside the man's house. Every time he left for the gambling-house, the dervish placed a stone to mark each sin upon a pile which he was accumulating as a visible reminder of evil.

Each time the other man went out he felt guilty. Each time he came back he saw another stone on the pile. Each time he put a stone on the pile the devotee felt anger at the gambler and personal pleasure (which he called 'Godliness') in having recorded his sin.

This process continued for twenty years. Each time the gambler saw the devotee, he said to himself:

'Would that I understand goodness! How that saintly man works for my redemption! Would that I could repent, let alone become like him, for he is sure of a place among the elect when the time of requital arrives!'

It so happened that, through a natural catastrophe, both men died at the same time. An angel came to take the soul of the gambler, and said to him, gently:

'You are to come with me to paradise.'

'But,' said the gambler, 'how can that be? I am a sinner, and must go to hell. Surely you are looking for the devotee, who sat opposite my house, who has tried to reform me for two decades?'

'The devotee?' said the angel, 'No, he is being taken to the lower regions, since he has to be roasted on a spit.'

'What justice is this?' shouted the gambler, forgetting his situation, 'you must have got the instructions reversed!'

'Not so,' said the angel, 'as I shall explain to you. It is thuswise: the devotee has been indulging himself for twenty years with feelings of superiority and merit. Now it is his turn to redress the balance. He really put those stones on that pile for himself, not for you.'

'And what about my reward, what have *I* earned?' asked the gambler.

'You are to be rewarded because, every time you passed the dervish, you thought first of goodness and secondly of the dervish. It is goodness, not man, which is rewarding you for your fidelity.'

THE SHEIKHS OF THE SKULLCAPS

Bahaudin Naqshband was approached by the sheikhs of four Sufi groups in India, Egypt, Turkey (Roum), and Persia. They asked him, in eloquently-worded letters, to send them teachings which they could impart to their followers.

Bahaudin first said: 'What I have is not new. You have it and do not use it correctly: therefore you will simply say when you receive my messages, "These are not new".'

The sheikhs replied: 'With respect, we believe that our disciples will not think thus.'

Bahaudin did not reply to these letters, but read them in his assemblies, saying: 'We at a distance will be able to see what happens. Those who are in the midst of it will not, however, make the effort to see what is happening to them.'

Then the sheikhs wrote to Bahaudin and asked him to give some token of his interest. Bahaudin sent one small skullcap, the *araqia*, for each student, telling their sheikhs to distribute them as from him, without saying what the reason might be.

He said to his assembly: 'I have done such-and-such

a thing. We who are far will see what those who are near to events will not see.'

Now he wrote, after a time, to each of the sheikhs, asking them whether they had abided by his wishes, and what the result had been.

The sheikhs wrote: 'We have abided by your wishes.' But as to the results, the sheikh of Egypt wrote: 'My community eagerly accepted your gift as a sign of special sanctity and blessing, and as soon as the caps were distributed each person regarded them as of the greatest inner significance, and as carrying your mandate.'

And the sheikh of the Turks wrote, on the other hand: 'The community regard your cap with great suspicion. They imagine that it betokens your desire to assume their leadership. Some are afraid that you may even influence them from afar through this object.'

There was a different result from the sheikh in India, who wrote: 'Our disciples are in great confusion, and daily ask me to interpret to them the meaning of the distribution of *araqias*. Until I tell them something about this, they do not know how to act.'

The letter from the sheikh of Persia said: 'The result of your distribution of the caps has been that the Seekers, content with what you have sent them, await your further pleasure, so that they may place at the disposal of their teaching and of themselves the efforts which should be made.'

Bahaudin explained to an audience of hearers in Bokhara:

'The dominant superficial characteristic of the people in the circles of India, Egypt, Turkey and Persia was in each case manifested by the reactions of their members. Their behaviour when faced with a trivial object such as

94

a skullcap would have been exactly the same if they had been faced with me in person, or with teachings sent by me. Neither the people nor their sheikhs have learned that they must look among themselves for their choking peculiarities. They should not use these trivial peculiarities as methods to assess others.

'Among the disciples of the Persian sheikh there is a possibility of understanding, because they have not the arrogance to imagine that they "understand" that my caps will bless *them*, will threaten *them*, will confuse *them*. The characteristics here are, in the three cases: Egyptian hope, Turkish fear and Indian uncertainty.'

Some of the epistles of Bahaudin Naqshband had meanwhile been copied as a pious act and distributed by well-meaning but unenlightened dervishes in Cairo, Hind and the Persian and Turki areas. They eventually fell into the hands of the circles surrounding these very 'Sheikhs of the Skullcaps'.

Bahaudin, therefore, asked one wandering Kalendar to visit each of these communities in turn, and to report to him how they felt about his epistles.

This man said on his return:

'They all said: "This is nothing new. We are doing all these things already. Not only that, but we are basing our daily lives on them, and by our existing tradition, we keep ourselves occupied day in and day out with remembrance of these things".'

El-Shah Bahaudin Naqshband thereupon called all his disciples together. He said to them:

'You who are at a distance from certain events connected with these four sheikhly groupings will be able to see how little has been accomplished by the working of the Knowledge among them. Those who are present there have learned so little that they can no longer profit from their own experiences. Where, therefore, is the advantage of the "daily remembrances and struggle"?

'Make it a task to collect all the available information about this event, inform yourselves of the whole story, including the exchange of letters and what I have said, as well as the report of this Kalendar here. Bear witness that we have offered the means whereby others could learn. Cause this material to be written down and studied, and let those who have been present witness it so that, God willing, even reading about it might prevent such things happening frequently in future, and might even enable it to come to the eyes and the ears of those who were so powerfully affected by the "action" of inactive skullcaps.'

THE SECRET OF THE LOCKED ROOM

Ayaz was the boon-companion and slave of the great conqueror Mahmud the Idol-Breaker, Monarch of Ghazna. He had first come to the court as a beggarly slave, and Mahmud had made him his adviser and friend.

The other courtiers were jealous of Ayaz, and observed his every movement, intending to denounce him for some shortcoming, thus encompassing his downfall.

One day these jealous ones went to Mahmud and said: 'Shadow of Allah upon Earth! Know that, indefatigable as always in your service, we have been keeping your slave Ayaz under close scrutiny. We have now to report that every day as soon as he leaves the Court, Ayaz goes into a small room where nobody else is ever allowed. He spends some time there, and then goes to his own quarters. We fear that this habit of his may be connected with a guilty secret: perhaps he consorts with plotters, even, who have designs upon your Majesty's life.'

For a long time Mahmud refused to hear anything against Ayaz. But the mystery of the locked room preyed upon his mind until he felt that he had to question Ayaz.

One day, when Ayaz was coming out of his private

chamber, Mahmud, surrounded by courtiers, appeared and demanded to be shown into the room.

'No,' said Ayaz.

'If you do not allow me to enter the room, all my confidence in you as trustworthy and loyal will have evaporated, and we can never thenceforward be on the same terms. Take your choice,' said the fierce conqueror.

Ayaz wept, and then he threw open the door of the room and allowed Mahmud and his staff to enter.

The room was empty of all furniture. All that it contained was a hook in the wall. On the hook hung a tattered and patched cloak, a staff and a begging-bowl.

The king and his court were unable to understand the significance of this discovery.

When Mahmud demanded an explanation, Ayaz said:

'Mahmud, for years I have been your slave, your friend and counsellor. I have tried never to forget my origins, and for this reason I have come here every day to remind myself of what I was. I belong to you, and all that belongs to me is my rags, my stick, my bowl and my wandering over the face of the earth.'

THE MIRACLE OF THE ROYAL DERVISH

It is related that the Sufi master Ibrahim ben Adam was sitting one day in a forest clearing when two wandering dervishes approached him. He made them welcome, and they talked of spiritual matters until it was dusk.

As soon as night fell, Ibrahim invited the travellers to be his guests at a meal. Immediately they accepted, a table laid with the finest foods appeared before their eyes.

'How long have you been a dervish?' one of them asked Ibrahim. 'Two years,' he said.

'I have been following the Sufi Path for nearly three decades and no such capacity as you have shown us has ever manifested itself to me,' said the man.

Ibrahim said nothing.

When the food was almost finished a stranger in a green robe entered the glade. He sat down and shared some of the food.

All realised by an inner sense that this was Khidr, the immortal Guide of all the Sufis. They waited for him to impart some wisdom to them.

When he stood up to leave, Khidr simply said:

'You two dervishes wonder about Ibrahim. But what have you renounced in order to follow the dervish Path?

'You gave up the expectations of security and an ordinary life. Ibrahim ben Adam was a mighty king, and threw away the sovereignty of the Sultanate of Balkh to become a Sufi. This is why he is far ahead of you. During your thirty years, too, you have gained satisfactions through renunciation itself. This has been your payment. He has always abstained from claiming any payment for his sacrifice.'

And next moment Khidr was gone.

ISHAN WALI'S TEST

Ishan Wali, when he suddenly appeared in Syria from Turkestan, showed that he had a remarkable range of techniques, (called by externalists his 'wisdoms') with which he was able to effect a forward movement in the then sluggish study of Sufism.

He found, for instance, that Sufi schools had become organisations bound together by traditionalism, and by regard for one master at the expense of the teachings of the Sufis as a whole. They worked with exercises and ideas which rightly belonged to other people, other times, and even other places.

The Wali's way of approaching this problem greatly impressed those who, while ignorant of his methods, believed that they should help him. They included Mustafa Ali Darazi, Ali-Mohammed Husseini and Tawil Tirmidhi, whose reports survive.

He told them:

'To the outward eye viewing these collections of people even by the reality that they have become flour-mills rather than schools, the ones to approach and the ones which have no capacity to learn are impossible to differentiate. I have, as you know, shown you that all are defective at present for the Work. But which of them is capable of revival?'

He pointed to a row of palm-trees which were suffering from the heat. 'If water is limited, which tree do we water? I have shown you that they are withered, something you did not realise before. Now I will show you a way to test whether individual trees may revive or not.'

Ishan Wali, as his demonstration, now met all the sheikhs of the repetitious Schools, most of whom welcomed him kindly, and indicated that they would be pleased to receive his help in re-establishing the Teachings.

He gave them no assurances. Separating himself from them, he then wrote to each one in the following vein:

'I have something of surpassing importance to say *to* you, and nothing at all to say *through* you. This means that I have to be permitted to address your followers directly. If you will allow this, I shall make my methods known. If, on the other hand, you do not allow it, I will be able eventually to address these people indirectly. But in that way you will have by refusal alienated yourself from me, and I will not be able to address myself *to* you. Since I have a responsibility either to all of you or to none, I cannot at the beginning use you as a channel when I am able to approach you directly. Since you have developed such a close affinity with your community, I must regard you as an essential member of the community, and cannot therefore treat you separately.'

He explained to his helpers that those sheikhs who were willing to regard themselves as pupils just as much as they regarded their own students as disciples, would be the ones who headed Schools which could be revivified.

Some sheikhs responded with understanding, and others

reacted with intense distrust, overtly or covertly, for Ishan Wali's approach.

Although he welcomed the understanding of the ones who regarded themselves as his pupils and as no different from their own smallest disciples in this respect, he grieved for the withered plants.

Ali-Mohammed Husseini said: 'Do we then sorrow for what has been shown to be dead?'

He answered: 'They are not all dead; it is only their suspicion that makes them behave as if they were dead.'

No sooner had he said this than some sheikhs of the divided schools, as if by innerly perceptive hearing, changed their attitudes and laid their turbans at his feet.

Majzub, one of the formerly perplexed sheikhs, said subsequently:

'I felt as if something oppressive had lifted, and I knew then that it was *my* fear and suspicion.'

But Ishan Wali said: 'It was the prayers of the "withering" sheikhs themselves, stronger than their fears and suspicions, which caused them to come to us and receive what we had to bring them. The merit is in fact all theirs. How can we have merit for doing something which we know? We have in the past earned merit for exercising virtues. But in this instance it is by pushing athwart their natures, full of rust, that *they* have polished the mirror of understanding.'

By this means did the suspicious sheikhs retain their importance in their own schools, and gain greater respect from their own disciples. The few who remained estranged found that their pupils were more and more inclining towards confusion of mind or adherence to the Wali, though he wrote to them to say:

'I do not enrol your pupils, not out of courtesy to you,

but because without the understanding of the whole body, the limb cannot function. If you fear loss of disciples through my presence, therefore, do not fear, for I cannot help them and will always say so. But I have fear for your eventual situation.'

The withered plants, except for a few, did not respond to this kindly rain. Today, of course, there is no trace on earth of the followers of those sheikhs which did not come to the methods of Ishan Wali during his Syrian residence.

HIDDEN MIRACLES

Someone asked Fuwad Ashiq, a senior disciple of Bahaudin Naqshband's:

'Can you tell me why it is that the Maulana conceals his miracles? I have often seen him in places when others have testified that they were with him at the time elsewhere. Similarly, when he cures someone by means of prayer, he may say, "It would have happened in any case". People who ask him favours, or who are favoured by his interest, gain great advantages in the world, but he denies his influence, or else attributes such events to coincidence or even to the work of others.'

Fuwad said:

'I have myself observed this many times; indeed, since I am so often with him it is now a matter of my daily experience. The reason is that miracles are the operation of "extraordinary service". They are not done to make people happy or sad. If they impress, this impressing is going to make the childish person credulous and excited, instead of making him learn something.'

ENTRY INTO A SUFI CIRCLE

If you read, if you practise, you may qualify for a Sufi circle. If you only read, you will not. If you think you have had experiences upon which you can build, you may not qualify.

Words alone do not communicate: there must be something prepared, of which the words are a hint.

Practice alone does not perfect humanity. Man needs the contact of the truth, initially in a form which will help him.

What is suitable and unexceptionable for one time and place is generally limited, unsuitable or a hindrance in another time and place. This is true in the search and also in many fields of ordinary life.

Hope and work so that you may be acceptable to a Sufi circle. Do not try to judge it or its members unless you are free from greed. Greed makes you believe things you would not normally believe. It makes you disbelieve things you should ordinarily believe.

If you cannot overcome greed, exercise it only where you can see it working, do not bring it into the circle of the initiates.

(Nazir el Kazwini, 'The Solitary Remarks')

A STORY OF IBN-HALIM

There were two men of great renown as teachers of the Right Path. Ibn Halim relates that he went first to see one of them, whose name was Pir Ardeshir of Qazwin.

He said to Pir Ardeshir: 'Will you advise me as to what to do and what not to do?'

The Pir said:

'Yes, but I will give you such instructions as you will find very hard to carry out, since they will go against your preferences, even if these preferences are sometimes for hardship.'

Ibn Halim spent some months with Pir Ardeshir, and found that the teaching was indeed hard for him. Although Pir Ardeshir's former disciples were now famed throughout the world as enlightened teachers, he could not stand the changes, the uncertainties and the disciplines placed upon him.

At length he applied to the Pir for permission to leave, and travelled to the tekkia of the second teacher, Murshid Amali.

He asked the Murshid: 'Would you place upon me burdens which I might find next to intolerable?'

Amali replied:

'I would not place upon you such burdens.'

Ibn Halim asked:

'Will you then accept me as a disciple?'

The Murshid answered:

'Not until you have asked me why my training would not be so onerous as that of Pir Ardeshir.'

Ibn Halim asked: 'Why would it not be so onerous?'

The Murshid told him: 'Because I would not care for you and your real wellbeing like Ardeshir cared for you. Therefore you must not now ask me to accept you as a disciple.'

THE WOMAN SUFI AND THE QUEEN

A certain woman of the disgraced family of the Omeyya
had become a Sufi, and she went to visit the Queen of
the household of El-Mahdi, who had replaced the
Omeyya.

The Queen was herself known as a woman of delicacy
and compassion. When she saw the emaciated and ragged
figure of the pauper Omeyyan princess at her door, she
asked her to come in, and prepared to give words of
comfort and such presents as would relieve her evident
want.

But no sooner had the Omeyyan princess said:

'I am a daughter of the Family of Omeyya...' than
the Queen forgot all her charity, and shouted:

'A woman of the accursed Omeyya! You have come,
no doubt, to beg for alms; forgetting what things your
menfolk did to our family, how they oppressed them and
treated them without mercy, leaving them no recourse
except for God ..'

'No,' said the Omeyyan princess, 'I did not come for
sympathy, forgiveness or money. I came to see whether
the family of El-Mahdi had learned to behave from their
predecessors, who could not: the ruthless sons of Omeyya,

or whether the conduct you deplore was a contagion which would certainly end in the downfall of those who contract it.'

The Omeyyan princess walked away and was not afterwards anywhere to be found.

But we have this story only from the words of the Queen of El-Mahdi, and so it may have been the cause of some improvement in human behaviour, somewhere.

THE COOK'S ASSISTANT

A certain famous, well-liked and influential merchant came to Bahaudin Naqshband. He said, in open assembly:

'I have come to offer my submission to you and to your teaching, and beg you to accept me as a disciple.'

Bahaudin asked him:

'Why do you feel that you are able to profit by the teaching?'

The merchant replied:

'Everything that I have known and loved in the poetry and the teaching of the ancients, as recorded in their books, I find in you. Everything that other Sufi teachers preach, extol and report from the Wise Ones I find in actuality in you, and not in completeness and perfection with them. I regard you as at one with the great ones, for I can discern the aroma of Truth in you and in everything connected with you.'

Bahaudin told the man to withdraw, saying that he would give him a decision as to his acceptability in due time.

After six months, Bahaudin called the merchant to him, and said:

'Are you prepared to appear publicly with me in an interchange?'

He answered:

'Yes, by my head and eyes.'

When a morning meeting was in progress, Bahaudin called the other man from the circle and had him sit beside him. To the hearers he said:

'This is so-and-so, the distinguished King of Merchants of this city. Six months ago he came here and believed that he could discern the aroma of truth in everything connected with me.'

The merchant said:

'This period of trial and separation, this six months without a glimpse of the Teacher, this exile, has caused me to plunge even more deeply into the classics, so that I could at least maintain some relationship with him whom I wish to serve, Bahaudin El-Shah, himself visibly identical with the Great Ones.'

Bahaudin said:

'Six moons have passed since you were last here. You have not been idle: you have been working in your shop, and you have been studying the lives of the Great Sufis. You could, however, have been studying me, whom you regard as identifiably one with the Knowers of the past, for I have been twice a week in your shop. During this six months during which we "have not been in contact", I have been forty-eight times in your shop. Many of those occasions passed with my making some kind of transaction with you, buying or selling merchandise. Because of the goods and because of a simple change of dress and appearance, you did not recognise me. Is this "discerning the aroma of truth"?'

The other man remained silent.

114

Bahaudin continued:

'When you come near to the man whom others call "Bahaudin", you can feel that he is the truth. When you meet the man who calls himself the merchant Khaja Alavi (one of Bahaudin's pseudonyms) you cannot discern the aroma of truth from that which is connected with Alavi. You find perceptibly in Naqshband only what others preach and themselves are not. In Alavi you do not find what the Wise are but do not appear to be. The poetry and the teaching to which you have referred is an outward manifestation. You feed on outward manifestation. Do not, please, give that the name of spirituality.'

This merchant was Mahsud Nadimzada, later a famous saint, who became a disciple of Bahaudin's after he had submitted to studying under the cook of the Khanqa, who was quite uninstructed in poetry, spiritual talk or exercises.

He once said:

'If I had not studied what I imagined to be a spiritual path, I would not have had to forget the numerous errors and superficialities which Khalifa-Ashpaz (the cook) burned out of me by ignoring my pretensions.'

WHY IS WET NOT DRY?

For thousands of years before he was known to people at large, Khidr travelled the earth looking for those whom he could teach.

When he found suitable students, he gave them truths and useful arts. But as often as he introduced new learning, it was appropriated and misused.

People cared only about the application of ability and laws, and not about understanding in depth, so knowledge could not develop as a whole.

So one day Khidr decided to apply a different means of learning. He made many things into their opposites. He made, for instance, what used to be wet into dry, and he made dry into wet.

People soon became used to this, and simply adjusted themselves to regarding wet as dry and dry as wet.

Having reversed an enormous number of things, Khidr will come back one day to show which is which again.

Until he does that, only a few will be able to benefit from Khidr's work. Those who do not are those who like to say: 'I knew that already,' when they did not.

BOOKS

If I give out an empty book, meaning, 'You cannot yet profit from my book', you will perhaps think, 'He is insulting me'.

But if I give out a full and understandable book, all readers will take its superficialities for their stimulation, exclaiming 'how magnificent, how profound'. People will follow these outward things after I am gone, making them a source of stimulation and debate. They will read didactics into them, or poetry, exercises or stories.

If I give out no books, or a small one, scholars will scoff and ruin the minds of potential and vulnerable students with alternative literature, even more than they do at present.

Baffled students become destructive, imagining solutions and then trying to impose them upon others.

If I give out a large book, some people will imagine that it is pretentious. All these suppositions are there, you notice, because they suit the people to have them, not because they are even likely to be true.

If I give out a cryptic book, people will imagine that it contains strange secrets. Or they may become unnecessarily artful through trying to understand it.

And the more that you say these things, the more people petulantly or with disdain say: 'You do not understand us. We have no such behaviour. The lack of understanding is with you.'

But if I say all these things, and you will look at all of them, even for a time, giving each statement equal attention, I shall be content.

(Bahaudin)

WHEN A MAN MEETS HIMSELF

One of man's greatest difficulties is also his most obvious drawback. It could be corrected if anyone troubled himself to point it out often and cogently enough.

It is the difficulty that man is describing himself when he thinks that he is describing others.

How often do you hear people say, about me:

'I regard this man as the Qutub (magnetic Pole) of the Age?'

He means, of course: '*I* regard this man...'

He is describing his own feelings or convictions, when what we might want to know is something about the person or thing being described.

When he says: 'This teaching is sublime,' he means: 'This appears to suit me.' But we might have wanted to know something about the teaching, not how he thinks it influences him.

Some people say: 'But a thing can truly be known by its effect. Why not observe the effect upon a person?'

Most people do not understand that the effect of, say, sunlight on trees is something constant. In order to know the nature of the teaching, we would have to know the nature of the person upon whom it has acted. The ordinary person cannot know this: all he can know is what that person assumes to be an effect upon himself – and he has no coherent picture of what 'himself' is. Since the outward observer knows even less than the person describing himself, we are left with quite useless evidence. We have no reliable witness.

Remember, that while this situation still obtains, there will generally be an equal number of people saying: 'This is marvellous,' as are saying: 'This is ridiculous'. 'This is ridiculous' really means: 'This appears ridiculous to me,' and 'this is marvellous' means: 'This appears marvellous to me.'

Do you really enjoy being like that?

Many people do, while energetically pretending otherwise.

Would you like to be able to test what really is ridiculous or marvellous, or anything in between?

You can do it, but not when you presume that you can do it without any practice, without any training, in the midst of being quite uncertain as to what it is you are and why you like or dislike anything.

When you have found yourself you can have knowledge. Until then you can only have opinions. Opinions are based on habit and what you conceive to be convenient to you.

The study of the Way requires self-encounter along the way. You have not met yourself yet. The only advantage of meeting others in the meantime is that one of them may present you to yourself.

Before you do that, you will possibly imagine that you have met yourself many times. But the truth is that when

you do meet yourself, you come into a permanent endow-
ment and bequest of knowledge that is like no other experience on earth.

(Tariqavi)

THE SUFI AND THE TALE OF HALAKU

A Sufi teacher was visited by a number of people of various faiths who said to him:

'Accept us as your disciples, for we see that there is no remaining truth in our religions, and we are certain that what you are teaching is the one true path.'

The Sufi said:

'Have you not heard of the Mongol Halaku Khan and his invasion of Syria? Let me tell you. The Vizier Ahmad of the Caliph Mustasim of Baghdad invited the Mongol to invade his master's domains. When Halaku had won the battle for Baghdad, Ahmad went out to meet him, to be rewarded. Halaku said: "Do you seek your recompense?" and the Vizier answered, "Yes".

'Halaku told him:

' "You have betrayed your own master to me, and yet you expect me to believe that you will be faithful to me." He ordered that Ahmad should be hanged.

'Before you ask anyone to accept you, ask yourself whether it is not simply because you have not followed the path of your own teacher. If you are satisfied about this, then come and ask to become disciples.'

FISH ON THE MOON

Sheikh Bahaudin Naqshband was asked:

'Why do you always say that none can learn Sufism by himself, and that nobody who thinks that he is more advanced in the Way than another is of any account at all?'

He answered:

'Because it is a matter of my daily experience that those who think that they can learn Sufism by themselves cannot in fact do so: they have too much self-centredness. Those who think that they cannot learn it alone can in fact do so. But, because of vanity, it is only a real Teacher who can give them leave to proceed alone, since he can diagnose their true condition.

'Whoever thinks that he is more advanced in Knowledge than another is almost completely ignorant, and is not able to learn further. He goes round and round in the "satan's intestines" of his ignorance. This is because the experience of real knowledge is in no way similar to thinking that one is more advanced than another.

'You observe that anyone whom I criticise for having self-will is never accepted by me as a pupil. This is because he would certainly feel, no matter what he imagined, that my criticism of him was motivated by a desire to teach him. Therefore those whom I criticise I always send away. There is always a hope that they might find a teacher somewhere who does not flatter them, though it is as likely as there are fish on the Moon.'

KILIDI AND THE GOLD PIECES

The Sufi teacher Kilidi found that many of his disciples spent much of their time spreading stories of his amazing virtues and his uncanny power of anticipating the thoughts and instructional needs of his pupils.

He reproached them for this time and again, but the human tendency to boast about someone whom one serves or admires was too strong for them. One day he said: 'Unless you stop this practice, which not only keeps me surrounded by sightseers but prevents me from imparting further significant knowledge to you, I will have to make an example which will cause you to dislike me. It could make you a laughing-stock for having followed me.'

Since this warning did not have the desired effect, Kilidi soon afterwards, in the presence of numerous disciples and members of the public, gave a hundred pieces of gold to a passing beggar.

Shortly afterwards the beggar came back with the gold, saying:

'This gold has done me no good. My wife now says that she should have half of it, or else that she should have an equal amount from you, since she is just as poor as I am.'

Kilidi took the gold and handed it to a rich man who was present, saying:

'Rich people don't complain of their money.'

He said to the beggar:

'Now you are restored to your former state, take up your normal harmonious relationship with your wife.'

Turning to his disciples, he said:

'Now you see that Kilidi makes mistakes, and the world has seen it as well.'

WHEAT AND BARLEY

A distinguished learned man who was visiting Bahaudin Naqshband asked:

'Through your character, exercises and manifest capacity for good, you are established in public, as in the hearts of your followers, as the current Master of the Age. Was it always thus with you?'

Bahaudin said:

'No, it was not always thus.'

The visitor said:

'The Ancients among the Sufis were frequently regarded as imitators, derided by scholars, feared by interpreters. Some of those whom the Adepts count as their most noble exemplars are registered in the books of the formally learned as undesirables or as influences not to be welcomed by the authorities. Yet if they have contributed to the knowledge and practice of the Way, they were surely visibly adepts?'

Bahaudin said:

'Some are evidently Adepts, others are evidently nothing.'

'Where then lies the essential quality of the dervish?'

'It lies in his reality, not in his appearance.'

'Have such people not qualities whereby everyone can assess them?'

Bahaudin answered :

'Remember the tale of the wheat and the barley. At one time people planted wheat in a field. Everyone became accustomed to seeing wheat come up, and to live on bread made from its flour. But time passed, and it was necessary to plant barley. When this came up many people, literalists as all ordinary scholars tend to be, cried out, "This is not wheat!"

' "Yes," said the growers of the barley, "but it is a cereal, and it is cereals which we all need."

' "Charlatan," cried the literalists. Many a time, when a barley crop was raised, the clamour to drive out the cultivators was so loud and effective that they were unable to provide flour for the people. The people starved, but they thought, persuaded by their literal-minded advisors, that they were better off avoiding the crop being cultivated by the barley-people.'

The visitor asked :

'Then what we call "Sufism" is really the cereal of your story? In that case we have been calling "wheat" or "barley" "cereals", and have to realise that there is something more profound of which both crops are a manifestation?'

'Yes,' said the Maulana.

'It would surely be more desirable if we could be given knowledge of "cereals" instead of "wheat" or "barley" under the name of "cereals", said the enquirer.

'It would surely be better if it could be done,' said Bahaudin, 'but the position is that most people, for their own sake and that of others, still have to work for the crop, so that they may eat. There are very few who know what cereals are. They are the people whom you call the Guides. When a man knows that people may die of starvation, he has to provide what food he can. It is only those who are not working in the fields who have time to wonder about grain. It is they, too, who have no right to do so, for they have not tasted it, nor are they working towards the production of flour for the people.'

'It is bad to tell people to do things when they cannot understand why they should do it,' said the visitor.

'It is worse to explain that a certain tree is going to fall in such detail that before you have finished the story your audience is crushed to death beneath it,' responded Bahaudin.

THE WINE FLASK

It is related in the assemblies of the Wise that there was once a man who wished to entertain a friend with the greatest hospitality of which he was capable.

When he and his friend had been sitting for some time after dining, the host said:

'Perhaps we should drink some wine, to stir the dullness of our thinking, and to stimulate the sharpness of our feelings?'

His guest agreed. Now that man had in his house only one flask of wine, and he told this to his guest. But when he sent his son, who was afflicted by the malady of double-vision, for the wine, he returned and said:

'Father, there are two bottles: which one of them do you want me to bring?'

Ashamed that his guest should think that he was not giving him his all, the father replied:

'Break the one bottle, and bring us here the other.'

The youth, of course, cast a rock upon the one and only bottle, with the result that he imagined that he had unintentionally broken both; and therefore there was no wine for host or guest that night.

The guest thought that the youth was a fool when he

was only suffering from a disability. The host's pride in his own hospitality was the cause of the destruction of the bottle. The boy was grieved that he had done something wrong.

This was all because the host was afraid that if he told his guest at the outset that his son was afflicted by double-vision, the guest would imagine that it was only a pretext for not being ready to expend all his wine.

SAID BAHAUDIN NAQSHBAND

We were standing on a small plateau in the high mountains of Kohistan.

My teacher said:

'Look at the conifers, how some are small and some are large. Some have rooted well, some lean awry. Others, for no evident reason, have some of their branches damaged.'

I said:

'What can we infer from this?'

He said:

'The tall ones are full of aspiration.'

'Are they all successful ones?'

'By no means.'

'And the damaged ones?'

'They are those who sought to justify themselves.'

'Are the small ones better than the tall?'

'Something may be small because of heredity, because of lack of opportunity, because of absence of nutrition, because of desire.'

'And the deep-rooted ones?'

'All depends upon their nature, and upon the selectivity

137

of their roots in gaining the real nourishment. Some deep-rooted ones are so because of an unnecessary greed to consume. Sometimes these are the ones which the woodsmen fell, and use for timber . . .'

THE SPONGE OF TROUBLES

It is related that for many centuries the tomb of Boland-Ashyan cured sicknesses, granted wishes, benefited all who visited it. It was known as 'The Sponge of Troubles'.

The shrine was situated near the small town of Murghzar in Iran, and here Faisal Nadim worked as a cook in the Ashkhana (restaurant) for twenty-odd years.

Faisal would never go to the shrine. But the travellers who entered his kitchen and spent time with him as he worked provided the line of Sufi illuminates called the Nadimis, and the visitors to the tomb were never celebrated as in any way sagacious except among the ignorant.

Someone asked the sage Khorram Ali why pious pilgrims were not transformed by their attendance at a place of such miracles – and why frequenters of a kitchen should become Sufi saints.

Khorram answered:

'A sponge sucks up water which is not needed, but it may also prevent, according to circumstances, useful work. It is quite insensitive, whatever merits you attribute to it. A cook knows the measure of ingredients and how to make them digestible. A cook may need a sponge to eliminate whatever stands in his way, such as dirty water. Only the stupid, looking only at the sponge, would imagine that it is working by its own volition.'

THE CRYSTAL FISH

A young man, having done a certain boatman a kindness, was presented by him with a tiny crystal fish.

He lost it and, in his despair at losing such a rare and beautiful object, was incensed when he saw another man around whose neck was a cord on which hung a crystal fish.

The youth took the man to court, and had him convicted of theft. At the last moment, when asked if he had anything to say before being conducted to prison, the man said:

'Ask any boatman of this country – we all have such emblems, and mine is my own. It does not belong to this youth. I have two eyes and a mouth too, but they are not his either!'

'Why did you not speak up before?' asked the magistrate of the boatman.

'Because there is more merit for all mankind if the truth is arrived at by the exercise of sense by all parties from the beginning, than if one has to prove something which might just, after all, not be capable of proof.'

'We must all learn, however,' remarked the judge.

'Alas!' said the boatman, 'if learning is considered to be

dependent upon the production of proof, we only have one-half of knowledge, and we are surely lost.'

The Kishtiwanis, to which School this boatman belonged, were noted for their habit of emphasising that people spend most of their time either jumping to conclusions or else taking no notice at all of facts.

THE SEAL BEARER

Very soon after the death of Maulana Bahaudin Naqshband, a ragged man arrived near his burial-place and demanded:

'Take me to the Khalifa (Deputy).' The Khalifa was not there.

He said: 'Let Bibi Jan, Maulana's widow, identify me.'

Everyone was nonplussed by the stranger, and those who remained of the Maulana's following did not know what to say or do.

The wanderer said:

'No Khalifa, no understanding! So I shall show you this, which even a man-donkey should know.'

He produced the seal of Bahaudin Naqshband.

Now this man was treated with honour, but he asked to be taken to the wall against the hill of Tillaju. He threw down a part of that wall, and told the men present to dig out its foundations.

Then he removed certain objects buried there and said:

'These are for me. They would have been for the disciples, if they had been Adepts.'

Someone asked:

143

'Why did the disciples not get them?'

He said:

'El-Shah told them to dig out the foundations of the wall, but instead they built the wall on top. So the wall will eventually fall, and the priceless objects here would have been lost. The idleness of the murids (disciples) in manual labour, and their superiority in imagination has caused their negation in the spiritual realm.'

A Murid asked:

'May we know of those who are not like us, for we crave knowledge.'

The mysterious dervish said:

'Those who could know already know. Those who are left are too late to know. They therefore satisfy themselves with having been near El-Shah. But it would be better if they were to disband. Otherwise they will merely repeat the names and formulae of El-Shah, and people will be led astray, imagining that this is Sufism.'

Someone said:

'Which Enlightened One are you, which Wali, which Abdal? Will you not stay with us?'

He answered:

'I am the lowest servant of the Masters, the Khwajagan. A servant can only stay where he can serve his master's commands. I cannot carry out the service of humility in the company of arrogance.'

Someone asked:

'How can we reduce our arrogance?'

He said:

'You can reduce it by realising that you are not worthy to be representatives of the Teaching of El-Shah. The unworthy are doubly incapacitated. They lead themselves astray by imagining that they are studying the Way.

They lead others astray by pretending to teach them, even by implication.

'This is not study. This is not teaching. Where there is no Representative, imitation of his position is equal to usurpation. Usurpation destroys the soul.'

FULL

An astronomer who was vain and full of his knowledge went on his travels and visited Kushyar the Sage, teacher of Avicenna.

But Kushyar would have nothing to do with him, and declined to teach him in any way.

The astronomer was taking his leave, in sadness, when Kushyar said:

'Your belief that you know so much has the effect of making you equal to a container completely full of water. Because of that, like the vessel, you are unable to admit any more.

'But the fullness is the repletion of vanity, and the fact is that you are really empty, no matter how you feel.'

VOICE IN THE NIGHT

A voice whispered to me last night:

'There is no such thing as a voice whispering in the night!'

(Haidar Ansari)

146

PERCEPTION

It is recorded that someone said to the great philosopher Saadi:

'I wish for perception, so that I shall become wise.'
Saadi said:

'Perception without wisdom is worse than nothing at all.'

He was asked: 'How can that be?'

Saadi said: 'As in the case of the vulture and the kite. The vulture said to the kite, "I have far better eyesight than you. Why, I can see a grain of wheat down there on the ground, while you see nothing at all."

'The two birds plummeted down to find the wheat, which the vulture could see and the kite could not. When they were quite near the ground the kite saw the wheat. The vulture continued his dive and swallowed the wheat. And then he collapsed: for the wheat was poisoned.'

SCRAPS

The scraps from the meal of the Emir are larger than the gifts of halwa from the merchant.

Timur Fazil

147

THE GOLDEN FLY

There was once a man called Salar, who knew right from wrong, and who knew what should be done and what should not be done, and who knew much of book-learning. He knew so much, in fact, that he had been appointed to be the personal assistant to the Mufti Zafrani, an eminent jurisconsult and judge.

But Salar did not know everything; and even in the things he did know, he did not always act in accordance with his knowledge.

One day, when he had set aside his glass of sweet juice, a tiny, shimmering golden fly settled on the rim and took a sip. Then the same thing happened the next day, and the next, until the fly grew in size and Salar could easily see him. But the fly had grown so slowly that Salar hardly noticed him at all.

Finally, after several weeks, Salar had been deep in study of a knotty legal problem when he looked up and realised that the fly seemed much larger than it should be. He brushed it away. The fly at once rose into the air, circled the glass, and flew away.

But it came back. When Salar's vigilance was relaxed, the fly would swoop down, sit on the rim of the glass, and drink as much as it could. As the days went by, the fly became larger and larger, and as it drank more and more it also started to look different.

First Salar flicked it away. Then he found that he had

to take a stick to hit it with. Sometimes, too, the fly started to look to him like something with a semi-human form. It was, of course, a Jinn, and not a fly at all.

Finally, Salar shouted at the fly; and, lo, it answered, saying: 'I do not take so very much of your drink, and besides, I am beautiful, am I not?'

Salar was first amazed, then afraid, and in the end completely confused.

He started to derive some pleasure from the visits of the fly, even though it was drinking some of his sherbet. He watched as the fly danced, he thought about it a great deal, he did less and less work, and – as the fly became larger, he found himself feeling weaker and weaker.

Salar was often in trouble with the Mufti, and so he pulled himself together and decided to make an end of the fly. Summoning up all his resolution, he hit it a violent blow, and it flew away, saying. 'You have wronged me, for I only wanted to be your friend, but I shall go, if that is what you want.'

Salar at first felt that he had got rid of the fly for good and all. He said to himself: 'I have beaten it, and that proves that I am more powerful than it, be it man or Jinn, fly or not.'

Then, when Salar had convinced himself that the whole matter was at an end, the fly appeared again. It had grown to an enormous size, and it descended from the ceiling like a shimmering lake in the form of a man.

Two huge hands reached out and grasped Salar's throat.

When the Mufti came to look for his assistant, he was lying strangled on the floor. The side wall of the house had collapsed with the Jinn's passing, and all that was there to mark his enormousness was a handprint on the whitewash, as large as the side of an elephant.

TAVERN PLEDGE

'It may be *said*: "They came in vain."
Let it not *be* that they came in vain.

We leave this, the bequest, to you;
We finished what we could, we left the rest to you.

Remember, this is work entrusted –
Remember, beloved, we shall meet again.'

Dervish Song

THE KNIFE

A wandering dervish ran to where a Sufi sat deep in contemplation, and said:

'Quick! We must do something. A monkey has just picked up a knife.'

'Don't worry,' said the Sufi, 'so long as it was not a *man*.'

When the dervish saw the monkey again he found, sure enough, that it had thrown the knife away.

(Kardan)

CARAVANSERAI

There was once a man named Muin, who was swindled
and betrayed in his youth by another man, called Halim,
an unusually greedy individual.

Muin said to himself: 'One day I shall be in a position
to pay this man back. I shall become rich, and his envy will
ruin him, especially if I deny him money!'

But the years passed and Muin did not become rich.
His lifetime's savings would only have kept a wealthy
man for a month. When he was forty he became ill and
physicians said that he had only a few weeks to live.

Now Muin had a Sufi perceptor – Daud, son of Zakaria
– and he asked him what he might do.

'To arouse envy is no part of a Sufi's work,' said Daud,
'for envy is a fatal rotting which kills a man by its feeding and it can be extirpated only with the greatest of
difficulty. The only method, in fact, is for the afflicted
one to practise intense and real generosity, and that he is
rarely willing to do. I can tell you this, and I leave the
rest to you: the envious corrode themselves by what they
think is true, not by the real truth.'

Muin pondered these words deeply. Then he sent for
his son, Aram, and said to him: 'I have very little to

leave you, but I believe that I can settle a debt and make provision for you by a judicious investment, if I do it now; so obey me in every detail. There is only a short span of life left to me.'

Aram, following his instructions to the letter, took all his father's savings and bought rich robes, some jewels, two beautiful houses, and much else. Then the father and son went to the most costly caravanserai near the villain's home and called him to them. Muin, weakened by exertion, was lying in bed. When he saw Halim, he said:

'I am probably on my death-bed, and you are the only person whom I know in this locality. I have a son, as you see, and to him I will impart a Sufi's secret which produced all the things which you see as my possessions. Look after this boy Aram, and he will tell you the secret at the correctly auspicious moment, which I have confided to him.'

Soon afterwards Muin died. Now Halim, who was quite rich, lavished presents on the boy and did everything to impress his kindness upon him, greedy for the Sufi's secret. He remained ever attentive in case the opportune moment for the transmission of the secret should occur.

But Muin had told Aram: 'Reveal the words of the Sufi to Halim if he has been generous enough to you, if you ever find that he is no longer greedy.'

So Aram watched Halim for years. Halim offered money, but never, somehow, gave as much as he offered.

Aram took what was given, and he even asked for more, both directly and through intermediaries, to discover whether there was any reluctance on Halim's part – and he found a great deal of that.

This process continued for several years. Halim suffered from fits of elation and depression, and started to interest himself in all kinds of diversions, such as gossip, to relieve the tensions of his life.

Then, one day, he was reading a Sufi book which said: 'To promise and not to fulfill prevents the transmission of Sufi secrets.' He suddenly remembered that he had not fulfilled all his promises to Aram. The same day he offered Aram the balance of the very large sum which he had originally said that he would donate to him.

Aram said: 'I am no judge of why you did this: but since it may be for the right reason, I will tell you the Sufi's secret now.' He told Halim what had passed between the Sufi and Muin.

Now Halim, his greed overcome by his admiration for the wisdom of the Sufi, said: 'Aram, I have no place in my heart for regret at the money which has been spent. Do just one thing for me – tell me how to find this Sufi, that I may kiss his feet.'

That is the story told by Halim, the great Sufi sage, who eventually succeeded Sheikh Daud, son of Zakaria.

FANTASIES

O man! If you only knew how many of the false fantasies of the imagination were nearer to the Truth than the careful conclusions of the cautious. And how these truths are of no service until the imaginer, having done his work with the imagination, has become less imaginative.

(Shab-Parak)

IRRELEVANCE

One of the Sufi sages appointed a deputy to transmit his instructions to disciples. Before long, however, the disciples took it on themselves to regard the deputy not as a channel but as a man of sanctity and authority. He, in turn, started to imagine that everything he said was significant. Presently, becoming doubtful of some of the results of the deputy's actions, some of the disciples enquired of one another: 'Is this man acting in full accord with his mandate?' Some of them regarded such thoughts as treachery, and blinded themselves to all abuses.

The Sage heard the questionings and answered: 'Vanity has taken possession of this deputy, but it has been nourished by your own desires to venerate someone.'

The disciples were crestfallen, and asked: 'If this can happen to a trusted representative, what might not happen in our case?'

The Sage told them: 'It could not have happened if both parties had not been to blame. If you had been obeying my orders, instead of creating your own imitation teacher, not satisfied with instructions and instead seeking idols, this would not have happened. But, on the other hand, where those tendencies are present, it not only does happen but must happen. Instead of wondering at what has taken place, you should observe how incapable you are of distinguishing the false from the true: though you are not humble enough not to assume that the false is the true.'

'That is your lesson.'

They said: 'What is to become of him?'

He answered: 'That is not your concern. It is concerning yourselves with the irrelevant which has hindered your development: and now you are still doing it. Far from being in advance of ordinary people, you are now far behind them. Do you want to catch up?'

FIDELITY

Najmaini ('The Man of the Two Stars') dismissed a student with the words: 'Your fidelity has been tested. I find it so unshakeable that you must go.'

The student said: 'Go I shall, but I cannot understand how fidelity can be a ground for dismissal.'

Najmaini said: 'For three years we have tested your fidelity. Your fidelity to useless knowledge and superficial judgments is complete. That is why you must go.'

THE SANCTUARY OF JOHN THE BAPTIST

Saadi, the Sufi author of the Persian classic *The Rose Garden*, writes of a visit to the burial-place of John the Baptist, in Syria.

He arrived there one day, exhausted and footsore. But then, as he was feeling sorry for himself, he saw a man who was not only tired, but had no feet. Saadi gave thanks to God that he, at least, had feet.

This story, on the obvious level, means 'be grateful for small mercies'. Its teaching on that level is found in all cultures. It is useful to help one to find a greater perspective in his situation if he is suffering from disabling self-pity.

The employment of such tales for emotional purposes – to switch the mental attitude, even to make a person content with and perhaps momentarily grateful for, his lot – is characteristic of the conventional type of instruction.

Modern sophisticates say: 'All that Saadi did was to inculcate so-called moral virtues – his work is outmoded.' Traditional, crude sentimentalists may say: 'How beautiful to dwell on the misery of others and one's own comparative good luck.'

But Saadi, being a Sufi, included in his writings materials which had more than one possible function. This tale is one of them.

In Sufi schools the piece is treated for what it is, an exercise. The student may benefit from whatever 'uplifting' moral may be the conventional interpretation. But, without introspection but with self-observation he should be able to say: 'I realise that changes in my mood are dependent on emotional stimuli. Do I always have to be dependent upon "seeing a man with no feet", or reading about it, before I realise that 'I have feet'? How much of my life is being wasted while I wait for someone to tell me what to do, or something to happen which will change my condition and frame of mind?'

According to the Sufis, man has better, more reliable, inner sense and capacities for educating them than constant emotional stimulus.

The object of the Sufi interpretation of this lesson would be nullified if it caused people to start an orgy of self-questioning of an emotional kind.

The purpose of pointing out this Sufi usage of the narrative is for it to be registered in the mind, so that the student may in future notice a higher form of assessment of his situation, when it begins to operate in him.

THE MEANING

A man who had spent many years trying to puzzle out meanings went to see a Sufi and told him about his search.

The Sufi said:

'Go away and ponder this – IHMN.'

The man went away. When he came back, the Sufi was dead. 'Now I shall never know the Truth!' moaned the puzzler.

At that moment the Sufi's chief disciple appeared.

'If,' he said, 'You are worrying about the secret mean- of IHMN, I will tell you. It is the initials of the Persian phrase *"In huruf maani nadarand"* – "These letters have no meaning." '

'But why should I have been given such a task?' cried the puzzling man.

'Because, when a donkey comes to you, you give him cabbages. That is his nutrition, no matter what he calls it. Donkeys probably think that they are doing something far more significant than eating cabbages.'

THE METHOD

A certain Sufi teacher was explaining how a false Sufi had been unmasked. 'A real Sufi sent one of his disciples to serve him. The disciple waited on the imposter hand and foot, day and night. Presently everyone began to see how the fraud loved these attentions, and people deserted him until he was completely alone.'

One of the listeners to this story said to himself: 'What a marvellous idea! I shall go away and do just the same thing.'

He went to where a bogus divine was to be found, and passionately desired to be enrolled as a disciple. After three years, such was his devotion that hundreds of devotees had collected. 'This sage must indeed be a great man' they said to one another, 'to inspire such loyalty and self-sacrifice in his disciple.'

So the man went back to the Sufi from whom he had heard the story and explained what had happened. 'Your tales are not reliable,' he said, 'because when I tried to put one into practice, the reverse happened.'

'Alas,' said the Sufi, 'there was only one thing wrong with your attempt to apply Sufi methods. You were not a Sufi.'

ABU TAHIR

Mir Abu Tahir attracted many students through his illuminating discourses and by circulating epistles which were favourably commented upon by all the major thinkers of the day.

When, however, people collected to hear him speak in person, they could only get him to repeat a single phrase:

'The desire for the merit, not for the man.'

This admonition was given out several times a day for five years. Someone went to the sage Ibriqi and begged him to help with some sort of explanation of the strange conduct of Abu Tahir.

Ibriqi said:

'You complain because the Mir says something regularly. But you do not complain that the sun raises and sets every single day. Yet the two things are the same. Like the sun, the Mir is doing something valuable. If you make no use of it, he must still continue to 'shine' for the benefit of those who *can* profit, or of you, at a time when you *can* benefit.'

CONTAINMENT

A dervish traveller recounts:

I visited a certain sheikh who was a magnet for people of the most miscellaneous character.

I said:

'How can you bear the company of such dreadful people! They have neither been improved by their proximity to you, nor were they attracted to you in the first place by your virtues, for by their own confession they seek only powers not possessed by other men.'

He said, and I shall never forget it:

'Friend, if all the snakes in the world were to be about their business of killing, and none was to be diverted by vain hopes which prevented his evil from being exercised, there would not be a single human being left alive.'

SIFTING

O Pedant! Sift, all your life, the writings and the sayings of the Wise. But first of all learn one thing: you are using a sieve which lets through chaff and discards the nutrient, the wheat.

(Shab-Parak)

THE PERFECT MASTER

A certain man decided that he would seek the Perfect Master.

He read many books, visited sage after sage, listened, discussed and practised, but he always found himself doubting or unsure.

After twenty years he met a man whose every word and action corresponded with his idea of the totally realised man.

The traveller lost no time. 'You,' he said, 'seem to me to be the Perfect Master. If you are, my journey is at an end.'

'I am, indeed, described by that name' said the Master.

'Then, I beg of you, accept me as a disciple.'

'That' said the Master, 'I cannot do; for while you may desire the Perfect Master, he, in turn, requires only the Perfect Pupil.'

GIVE AND TAKE

The Chief takes less then he is given
And gives more than he has taken.

(Kitab-i-Amu Daria)

THE FOX'S PROOF

Once upon a time there was a fox who met a young rabbit in the woods. The rabbit said: 'What are you?' The fox said: 'I am a fox, and I could eat you up if I wanted to.'

'How can you prove that you are a fox?' asked the rabbit. The fox didn't know what to say, because in the past rabbits had always run from him without such enquiries.

Then the rabbit said: 'If you can show me written proof that you are a fox, I'll believe you.'

So the fox trotted off to the lion, who gave him a certificate that he was a fox.

When he got back to where the rabbit was waiting, the fox started to read out the document. It so pleased him that he dwelt over the paragraphs with lingering delight. Meanwhile, getting the gist of the message from the first few lines, the rabbit ran down a burrow and was never seen again.

The fox went back to the lion's den, where he saw a deer talking to the lion. The deer was saying:

'I want to see written proof that you are a lion...'

The lion said:

'When I am not hungry, I don't need to bother. When I *am* hungry, you don't need anything in writing.'

The fox said to the lion: 'Why didn't you tell me to do that, when I asked for the certificate for the rabbit?'

'My dear friend,' said the lion, 'you should have said that it was requested by a rabbit. I thought it must be for a stupid human being, from whom some of these idiotic animals have learned this pastime.'

OPPORTUNITY

The words 'You have a chance,' from the lips of the Authority, are worth more than a hundred times 'You are the greatest man in the world' from the fool.

(Nuri Falaki)

THE LOAN

A man was telling his friends in a teahouse:

'I lent someone a silver piece, and I have no witnesses. Now I am afraid that he will deny that he ever had anything from me.'

The friends commiserated, but a Sufi who was sitting in the corner raised his head from his knee and said:

'Invite him here and mention in conversation, in front of these people, that you lent him twenty gold pieces.'

'But I only lent him one silver piece!'

'That,' said the Sufi, 'is exactly what he will shout out – and everyone will hear him. You did want witnesses, did you not?'

LIGHT-WEAVING

They asked Firmani:

'How did you know that such-and-such a man was vicious? You refused to converse deeply with him while he was here, although everyone said that he was a saint.'

Firmani said:

'If a stranger comes to ordinary men and says "Light is made by weaving. I wove all the light there is and was," what do they realise?'

They answered:

'They realise that what he says is untrue.'

Firmani said:

'Similarly, when a vicious individual enters the company of a man of knowledge, it is not difficult to judge his condition, regardless of what people imagine or say.'

EXPLANATION

The assumption that anyone of worth can explain himself fully and lucidly in the time allotted him by those who want to learn what he knows – is either a joke or a stupidity.   (Shab-Parak)

DAY AND NIGHT

A scholar said to a Sufi:

'You Sufis often say that our logical questions are incomprehensible to you. Can you give me an example of what they seem like to you?'

The Sufi said:

'Here is such an example. I was once travelling by train and we went through seven tunnels. Opposite me was sitting a peasant who obviously had never been in a train before.

'After the seventh tunnel, the peasant tapped me on the knee and said:

' "This train is too complicated. On my donkey I can get to my village in only one day. But by train, which seems to be travelling faster than a donkey, we have not yet arrived at my home, though the sun has risen and set seven whole times." '

SOURCE OF BEING

Allow the Source of Being to maintain contact with you: ignore the impressions and opinions of your customary self. If this self were of value in your search, it would have found realisation for you. But all it can do is to depend upon others. (Amin Suhrawardi)

STAINED

It is related that a man went to the assembly of the master Baqi-Billah of Delhi and said:

'I have been reading the famous verse of the Master Hafiz, "If your teacher bids you stain your prayer-carpet with wine, obey him," but I have a difficulty.'

Baqi-Billah said:

'Dwell apart from me for some time and I shall illustrate the matter for you.'

After a considerable period of time, the disciple received a letter from the sage. It said: 'Take all the money you have and give it to the gate-keeper of any brothel.'

The disciple was shocked, and for a time thought that the master must be a fraud. After wrestling with himself for days, however, he went to the nearest house of ill-fame and presented the man at the door with all the money which he had.

'For such a sum of money' said the doorman, 'I shall allot you the choicest gem of our collection, an untouched woman.'

As soon as he entered the room, the woman there said:

'I have been tricked into being in this house, and am held here by force and threats. If your sense of justice is stronger than your reason for coming here, help me to escape.'

Then the disciple knew the meaning of the poem of Hafiz, 'If your teacher bids you stain your prayer-carpet with wine, obey him.'

WAHAB IMRI

A man went to Wahab Imri and said:

'Teach me humility.'

Wahab answered:

'I cannot do that, because humility is a teacher of itself. It is learnt by means of its practice. If you cannot practise it, you cannot learn it. If you cannot learn it, you do not really want to learn it inwardly at all.'

THE ROGUE AND THE DERVISH

A certain dervish planned an object lesson. He paid an actor to go to a town and set himself up as a religious teacher. 'Collect all the disciples you can' he said, 'pretending to be a man of great sanctity. When I arrive, I shall unmask you. The people will realise that they have been fooled, and will listen to my teachings, once I have shown them how shallow are their beliefs.'

Some months later the dervish entered the town and made his way to the mystic's house. There was the actor, surrounded by adoring disciples who were showering him with gifts and praising his every word.

The dervish started to speak:

'O people! Know that I have come to explain everything to you. I sent this man to prove how people will believe anything if they want to. Now I shall give you true teaching instead.'

The actor said nothing at all. The people seized the dervish and carried him off to an asylum as a madman. The actor came to the barred window one night and said to him: 'Although a vagabond in appearance I was wise enough to accept your advice. Although a wise man in your own opinion, you were foolish enough to believe in your own plans. A crooked plan will benefit only the crooked, and a wise one only the wise.'

HOPE

There was once a king, descended from a long and powerful line, whom adversity had driven from his position, and who was in flight before his enemies.

The king was soaked to the skin by rain and, in the middle of a desolate moor, came across a small hut used by shepherds. He thought that he would rest there for a little, and when he went inside he found that there were two shepherds already there, wrapped in blankets against the cold.

They welcomed him kindly, and shared their only food, some cheese and onions, with him.

The king said:

'One day, when I am restored to sovereignty, I shall repay you in the coin of a king!'

Now, although both shepherds had offered the king food and were therefore equally generous, they were not both possessed of equal qualities in every way.

The first shepherd, therefore, strutted about telling everyone that he was better even than a nobleman, for he had given food to a king when there was nobody else to do so.

But the second shepherd, on reflection, said to himself:

'My being in the hut, and my having some food with me, were accidents. My offering food to the king was a normal action. But the king, with truly royal generosity, chose to interpret these facts as the result of merit. Now it is for me to be inspired by this example, and to make myself truly worthy of such high-mindedness.'

Two or three years later the king returned to his rightful power, and he sent for the shepherds. Each of them was given rich gifts and both obtained powerful positions at court.

But the first shepherd, not having exerted any efforts to improve and prepare himself, soon fell a victim to an intrigue, and he was put to death for plotting. The second shepherd, on the other hand, worked so well that when the king reached a great age, he was nominated and accepted as his successor.

WANTING

If you want to be with the Teacher when he wants you to be apart from him, you must obey him or shun him. If you argue about it, you are worse than disobedient.

(Halqavi)

THE ARCHER

The champion bowman of the town of Salimia complained that he had no peer.

'These people, the Salimites, are no archers, and thus they cannot judge my excellence!' He repeated, again and again, to anyone who would listen.

He convinced everyone of his unhappiness.

One day a certain Sufi master was passing through the town, and stopped to drink some tea.

In the teahouse the people told him of the miserable archer.

'He may believe that he is suffering' said the sage, 'but the All-Highest has in fact been more than kind to this man. Had he been placed among archers, he would have been in constant fear of being outdone.

'If he had really needed adversaries of his own quality, nothing would have prevented him from finding them.

'Until man – and his audience – can hear the unspoken message, and forget the spoken one, he will remain in chains.'

MAHMUD AND THE DERVISH

It is related that Mahmud of Ghazna was once walking in his garden when he stumbled over a blind dervish sleeping beside a bush.

As soon as he awoke, the dervish cried:

'You clumsy oaf! Have you no eyes, that you must trample upon the sons of men?'

Mahmud's companion, who was one of his courtiers, shouted:

'Your blindness is equalled only by your stupidity! Since you cannot see, you should be doubly careful of whom you are accusing of heedlessness.'

'If by that you mean,' said the dervish, 'that I should not criticise a sultan, it is you who should realise your shallowness.'

Mahmud was impressed that the blind man knew that he was in the presence of the king, and he said mildly:

'Why, O Dervish, should a king have to listen to vituperation from you?'

'Precisely,' said the dervish, 'because it is the shielding of people of any category from criticism appropriate to them which is responsible for their downfall. It is the burnished metal which shines most brightly, the knife struck with the whetstone which cuts best, and the exercised arm which can lift the weight.'

STAGES

First I thought that a Teacher must be right in all things.

Then I imagined that my teacher was wrong in many things.

Then I realised what was right and what was wrong.

What was wrong was to remain in either of the first two states.

What was right was to convey this to everyone.

(Ardabili)

WHAT IS IN IT

A certain Bektashi dervish was respected for his piety and appearance of virtue. Whenever anyone asked him how he had become so holy, he always answered: 'I know what is in the Koran.'

One day he had just given this reply to an enquirer in a coffee-house, when an imbecile asked: 'Well, what *is* in the Koran?'

'In the Koran,' said the Bektashi, 'there are two pressed flowers and a letter from my friend Abdullah.'

SOUND AND UNSOUND

A wandering Seeker saw a dervish in a rest-house and said to him:

'I have been in a hundred climes and heard the teachings of a multitude of mentors. I have learned how to decide when a teacher is not a spiritual man. I cannot tell a genuine Guide, or how to find one, but half the work completed is better than nothing.'

The dervish rent his garments and said:

'Miserable man! Becoming an expert on the useless is like being able to detect rotten apples without learning the characteristics of the sound ones.

'But there is a still worse possibility before you. Beware that you do not become like the doctor in the story. In order to test a physician's knowledge, a certain king sent several healthy people to be examined by him. To each the doctor gave medicine. When the king summoned him and charged him with this deceit, the leech answered: 'Great King! I had for so long seen nobody but the ailing that I had begun to imagine that everyone was ill and mistook the bright eyes of good health for the signs of fever!'

LAMB STEW

Bahaudin Shah once gave an address on the principles
and practices of the Sufis. A certain man who thought
that he was clever and could benefit from criticising him,
said:

'If only this man would say something new! That is
my only criticism.'

Bahaudin heard of this, and invited the critic to dinner.

'I hope that you will approve of my lamb stew,' he said.

When he had taken the first mouthful, the guest jumped
up, shouting, 'You are trying to poison me – this isn't
lamb stew!'

'But it *is*,' said Bahaudin, 'though, since you don't like
old recipes, I have tried something new. This contains
lamb all right, but there is a good dash of mustard, honey
and emetic in it as well.'

FINDING FAULT

Isa Ibn Abdulwahab al-Hindi held long and frequent con-
versations in which he discoursed on every imaginable
topic, for a number of years.

One day a certain respected Sheikh called upon him
and said:

'My heart is heavy, for it is reported that you have
spoken critically of me on many occasions.'

Isa said:

'I have said twenty times that there are disparities between your words and actions. Can you doubt that this is
true?'

The sheikh asked:

'I would be glad to hear the grounds upon which you
find fault with me.'

Isa replied:

'You will know them the moment you hear the two
hundred occasions on which I have praised you before
those same people who, in the name of accuracy, now
inwardly seek to separate us. To report half a thing
is worse than reporting nothing. To report one-tenth of
a thing is equal to falsification.'

HEARING

A visitor who had come from a far country said to Bahaudin Shah:

'Let me sit in your durbar and hear your words, for it has truly been said that reading is no substitute for hearing.'

Bahaudin said:

'Alas! If you are not deaf, it is sad that I should have had to wait so long to welcome you here. You see, I never give any lectures nowadays.'

The visitor asked why.

Bahaudin said:

'I have never given any lecture since a group of partially deaf people came one day. I said "Do not be like a dog or a swine..." and after they left me they fell out, disputing as to whether I had said "Be a dog..." or even "Eat swine's flesh..." With the written word this is not possible. If you are blind, someone can always read to you.'

THE BABY ELEPHANT

Once upon a time there was a baby elephant who heard someone say: 'Look, there is a mouse.' The person who said it was looking at a mouse – but the elephant thought that he was referring to him.

Now, there were very few mice in that country; and in any case they tended to stay in their holes, and their voices were not very loud. But the baby elephant thundered around, ecstatic at his discovery, 'I am a mouse!'

He said it so loudly and so often, and to so many people that – believe it or not – there is now an entire country where almost everyone believes that elephants, and particularly baby elephants, are mice.

It is true that from time to time mice have tried to remonstrate with those who hold the majority belief: but they have always been put to flight.

And if anyone ever wants to reopen the question of mice and elephants in those parts, he had better have a good reason, strong nerves and an effective means of putting his case.